Spelunking Scripture:
The Letters of Paul
Exploring Important Passages of the Bible

BRUCE C. SALMON

© 2021
Published in the United States by Nurturing Faith, Macon, GA.
Nurturing Faith is a book imprint of Good Faith Media (goodfaithmedia.org).
Library of Congress Cataloging-in-Publication Data is available.

ISBN: 978-1-63528-149-1

All rights reserved. Printed in the United States of America.

All scripture citations are from the New Revised International Version (NRSV) unless otherwise indicated.

Contents

Introduction v

Chapter 1: Not Ashamed of the Gospel 1
    Faith Alone (Rom. 1:16-17) 2
    Live by Faith (Rom. 1:16-17) 4
    Coming to Faith (Rom. 1:16-17) 6

Chapter 2: Sighs Too Deep for Words 9
    Too Deep for Words (Rom. 8:26-27) 10
    When the Sky Is Silent (Rom. 8:28) 12
    All Things Work Together for Good (Rom. 8:26-28) 15

Chapter 3: Nothing Can Separate Us 19
    Eucatastrophe (Rom. 8:28-39) 19
    Master of My Fate (Rom. 8:28, 31-39) 22
    Swinging in the Rain (Rom. 8:31-39) 25

Chapter 4: Not Conformed, But Transformed 29
    Transformed, Not Conformed (Rom. 12:1-2) 29
    Countercultural Christianity (Rom. 12:1-2) 32
    A Serious Call to a Devout and Holy Life (Rom. 12:1-2) 34

Chapter 5: The Lord's Supper 39
    Examine Yourselves (1 Cor. 11:23-28) 40
    We're in This Together (1 Cor. 11:17-28) 43
    A Life Worthy (1 Cor. 11:23-28) 45

Chapter 6: The Love Chapter 49
    The Greatest Is Love (1 Cor. 13:4-7, 13) 49
    The Greatest Gift (1 Cor. 13:4-7, 13) 52
    It's All About Love (1 Cor. 13:4-8, 13) 54

Chapter 7: We Do Not Lose Heart 59
    Earthen Vessels (2 Cor. 4:7-18) 59
    Living in the Light of Eternity (2 Cor. 4:16-18) 62
    Live Like You Were Dying (2 Cor. 4:16-18) 65

Chapter 8: All God's Children 69
- The Great Equalizer (Gal. 3:26-29) 70
- The Social Gospel (Gal. 3:23-26) 71
- Created Equal (Gal. 3:26-28) 74

Chapter 9: Christian Freedom 79
- Freedom in Christ (Gal. 5:1, 13-14) 79
- John Leland: Freedom Preacher (Gal. 5:1) 82
- Freedom and Responsibility (Gal. 5:1, 13-14) 86

Chapter 10: Imitate Christ 89
- Christ-Minded (Phil. 2:5-11) 89
- He Humbled Himself (Phil. 2:5-11) 91
- Overcoming Pettiness (Phil. 2:3-11) 93

Chapter 11: Clothe Yourselves With Love 97
- One in the Spirit (Col. 3:12-15) 97
- The People of God (Col. 3:12-14) 100
- Where Healing Begins (Col. 3:12-17) 102

Chapter 12: All Scripture Is God-Breathed 107
- Back to School (2 Tim. 3:10-17) 107
- Rightly Dividing the Word of Truth (2 Tim. 2:15, 3:14-17) 110
- John Wycliffe: Scripture Alone (2 Tim. 3:14-17) 113

About the Author 117

Introduction

It was a Saturday, June 23, 2018. The Wild Boars soccer team had finished their practice, and 12 of the boys, ages 11 to 16, along with their 25-year-old assistant coach, rode their bikes to the Tham Luang Nang Non cave system in northern Thailand. Most of them had been inside the cave before, but they wanted to explore it further as a group. They ignored the sign outside the entrance of the cave, warning against entering during the rainy season, July through November. Shortly after they had entered, heavy rains began to fall, partially flooding the cave and trapping the group inside.

Later that day, parents began calling the head coach to report that their children had not come home from soccer practice. After the coach checked his phone and saw about 20 missed calls, he began calling the assistant coach and many of the players, but to no avail. Finally, he reached a team member who had been picked up after practice, and who said that the rest of the boys had gone exploring in the Tham Luang cave. The head coach rushed to investigate, and he found bags and bicycles outside the entrance to the cave, but no boys or their assistant coach. He alerted the local authorities that the group was missing. The next day, handprints and footprints of the boys were discovered by officials. A day after that, Thai Navy SEAL divers entered the cave to search for the missing team members.

The divers could go only so far into the cave system until they were stymied by floodwaters. American and British military divers were sent to Thailand to help with the search. They entered the cave but were repelled by more flooding. Then, heavy rains halted the rescue operation temporarily. Pumps were delivered to extract some of the water from the cave passages. After a brief pause in the rainfall, the search resumed. Finally, on the night of July 2, British divers found the team stranded inside the cave on an elevated ledge about two and a half miles from the entrance. The team members had stayed hydrated by licking condensed water from the cave walls. Their assistant coach, who had trained at a Buddhist monastery, led the boys in meditation exercises to stay calm. Although weak and hungry, they were still alive.

The rescue operation took another eight days. Divers delivered food, water, and medical supplies and an air tube to provide oxygen. Incredibly, all the boys and their assistant coach were delivered to safety. Tragically, a member of the rescue team perished. A 38-year-old Thai volunteer diver lost consciousness and died as he was bringing oxygen tanks into the cave.

Spelunking, or exploring underground passages in cave systems, is a popular pastime in many parts of the world. It can be exciting, but it also can be dangerous, especially without a trained guide. The assistant coach later apologized for acting without permission and leading the boys into a perilous situation.

Spelunking scripture, or exploring passages of the Bible, can be exciting, but it also can be dangerous. Frankly, exploring some passages of the Bible without a trained guide can lead to all sorts of dead ends and misinterpretations and unfortunate outcomes.

For example, some passages of the Bible have been (mis)used to justify slavery, the subjugation of women, and the condemnation of persons of a different sexual orientation. Misinterpreting passages of scripture can lead to bad theology and, even worse, practical abuses that negatively affect the lives of people.

JUSTIFICATION OF SLAVERY

As a two-time graduate of the Southern Baptist Theological Seminary, I was dismayed to learn that two founding faculty members of the seminary, John A. Broadus and James P. Boyce, were slaveowners.

Broadus was an outstanding preacher and New Testament scholar. His textbook for homiletics, *On the Preparation and Delivery of Sermons*, is still in print and in use in evangelical colleges and seminaries. The renowned British Baptist pastor Charles Spurgeon called Broadus "the greatest living preacher." Boyce was a systematic theologian who served as the first president of Southern Seminary. His text, *Abstract of Systematic Theology*, was widely used. Broadus and Boyce were among the most acclaimed Baptist leaders of their era. Yet, both owned slaves. In fact, Boyce, owner of 23 slaves at the beginning of the Civil War, described himself as "ultra pro slavery."[1] Boyce served as a chaplain in the Confederate army before being elected to the South Carolina legislature. Broadus also served as a chaplain in the Confederate army. In 1886 Broadus declared in an address at Cave Hill Cemetery in Louisville that fallen Confederate soldiers had not died in vain.[2]

How could Broadus and Boyce possibly have defended slavery? Like many southern preachers of their era, they found warrant for slavery in selected passages of scripture. Alexander McClain, a Methodist minister, wrote a pamphlet that argued slavery was ordained by God. After having read the pamphlet, John C. Calhoun, then vice president of the United States, wrote: "My Dear Sir, I have read with pleasure your pamphlet, entitled, '*Slavery Defended from the Scriptures Against Abolitionists*.' You have fully and ably made good that title. You have shown beyond all controversy that slavery is sanctioned both by the Old and New Testament."[3]

The Bible does have a lot to say about slavery. Slavery was common in the Old Testament. Abram and his wife Sarai were slaveowners. According to Genesis 16, Sarai instructed Abram to impregnate her slave Hagar. Today, we would call this act "rape." Such was the fate of some slaves in the Old Testament. In the New Testament, 19 of the 27 books mention slavery, and some passages explicitly command slaves to obey their masters. Consider these words from the apostle Paul:

> Slaves, obey your earthly masters with respect and fear, and with sincerity of heart, just as you would obey Christ. (Eph. 6:5 NIV)

> Slaves, obey your earthly masters in everything; and do it, not only when their eye is on you and to curry their favor, but with sincerity of heart and reverence for the Lord. (Col. 3:22 NIV)

All who are under the yoke of slavery should consider their masters worthy of full respect, so that God's name and our teaching may not be slandered. (1 Tim. 6:1 NIV)

Teach slaves to be subject to their masters in everything, to try to please them, not to talk back to them. (Titus 2:9 NIV)

Paul was not the only New Testament writer who told slaves to obey their masters. In 1 Peter 2:18 we read: "Slaves, in reverent fear of God submit yourselves to your masters, not only to those who are good and considerate, but also to those who are harsh" (NIV).

So, using these and other selected scripture passages, many southern preachers—including some esteemed Baptist seminary professors—defended the institution of slavery as ordained by God. How could they have so missed the mark?

Their biblical interpretation was a matter of failing to distinguish between the cultural conditions of the time and God's eternal intentions for human life. Slavery was a cultural condition of many parts of the ancient world, as reflected in the Old and New Testaments. But not every cultural institution was God-ordained.

Jesus gave us a clear picture of God's intentions for our lives, saying that, above all, we are to love God, and we are to love our neighbors as we love ourselves. There is no way that slavery can be squared with loving our neighbors as we love ourselves.

Despite his admonitions for slaves to obey their masters, Paul may have grasped a little of the incompatibility of slavery with love for neighbor. In his letter to Philemon, he urged the slaveowner to welcome back his escaped slave Onesimus. Paul did not challenge the institution of slavery, nor did he request that Onesimus be emancipated, although he may have hinted at it. Paul sent Onesimus back to his master, as the law required, but Paul did ask Philemon to accept Onesimus back into the household as "no longer a slave but more than a slave, a beloved brother ... in the Lord" (Phlm. 16, NRSV).

It took a long time, but eventually most Christians came to realize that slavery is abhorrent to the will of God. Rather than merely quoting those few isolated passages in Paul's letters and 1 Peter that admonish slaves to obey their masters, most Christians came to see the bigger picture of God's design for human community. God wants us to love each other, not to enslave each other. But the legacy of slavery is still with us, namely, in the racism upon which slavery in the American experience was based.

SUBJUGATION OF WOMEN

In many cultures in the ancient world, and in many cultures even into the 21st century, women have been suppressed and treated as inferior to men. For example, women did not gain suffrage in the United States until 1920 with the passage of the 19th Amendment to the Constitution. In many other countries, women did not gain the right to vote until even later in the 20th century. Women continue to be treated as inferior to men in many other ways. How did that come about? Once again, it was a cultural condition in many societies. And throughout much of Christian history, the Bible has been used to subjugate women.

In the first account of creation in Genesis 1, male and female are created together in the image of God: "Then God said, 'Let us make humankind in our image, according to our likeness, and let them have dominion over the fish of the sea, and over the birds of the air, and over the cattle, and over all the wild animals of the earth, and over every creeping thing that creeps upon the earth, so God created humankind in his image, in the image of God he created them, male and female he created them" (vv. 26-27 NRSV).

There is no suggestion in the first creation account in Genesis 1 that women are inferior to men. The second creation account in Genesis 2, however, has been misinterpreted to imply male superiority: "then the Lord God formed man from the dust of the ground, and breathed into his nostrils the breath of life, and the man became a living being … Then the Lord God said, 'It is not good that the man should be alone; I will make him a helper as his partner'" (vv. 7, 18 NRSV). This idea that the man was created first, and that the woman was created after him to be his helper, led some interpreters to conclude that the man was superior to the woman. Some misunderstood the meaning of the term, "helper." According to Old Testament scholar Tony Cartledge, "the word usually translated as 'helper' *('ezer)* does not describe an aide or a maid…. in the Old Testament the word is used of God acting as a deliverer or protector or sustainer, the one who does what man alone cannot do. The woman is not inferior to the man but corresponds to him. She is not below him but beside him. She is not a servant but a partner; not a subordinate but an equal."[4]

In the story of the Fall in Genesis 3, the serpent approaches the woman and tempts her to eat the forbidden fruit. She takes some and eats it, then gives some to her husband. When God questions the man about eating the forbidden fruit, the man blames the woman for giving it to him. When the Lord God questions the woman, she blames the serpent for deceiving her. So, the serpent and the woman and Adam all suffer consequences for what they have done. Adam and his wife are banished from the Garden of Eden. Some interpreters (including Paul in 1 Timothy 2) make the woman subservient because she was the first to sin. Genesis 3:16, "he shall rule over you," has been used as a justification for husbands ruling over their wives. This (mis)interpretation argues that female submission is ordained by God.

In Genesis 19 we find a story about Lot, his wife, and their two daughters who are living in Sodom. Two angels arrive at Sodom, and Lot offers them hospitality. Later that evening their house is surrounded by the men of Sodom who demand that Lot send out his visitors so the men can "have sex with them" (v. 5, NIV). Lot replies, "No, my friends. Don't do this wicked thing. Look, I have two daughters who have never slept with a man. Let me bring them out to you, and you can do what you like with them. But don't do anything to these men, for they have come under the protection of my roof" (vv. 7-8, NIV). Such was the status of women in the Old Testament. Lot offered his daughters to be raped by the men of Sodom to try to protect his (male) guests.

Several passages in the New Testament have been used to make women seem subject and inferior to men, for example:

Introduction

> Women should remain silent in the churches. They are not allowed to speak, but must be in submission, as the law says. If they want to inquire about something, they should ask their own husbands at home; for it is disgraceful for a woman to speak in the church. (1 Cor. 14:34-35 NIV)

> A woman should learn in quietness and full submission. I do not permit a woman to teach or to assume authority over a man; she must be quiet. For Adam was formed first, then Eve. And Adam was not the one deceived; it was the woman who was deceived and became a sinner. (1 Tim. 2:11-12 NIV)

> Wives, in the same way submit yourselves to your own husbands, so that, if any of them do not believe the word, they may be won over without words by the behavior of their wives. (1 Pet. 3:1 NIV)

> Husbands, in the same way be considerate as you live with your wives, and treat them with respect as the weaker partner and as heirs with you of the gracious gift of life, so that nothing will hinder your prayers. (1 Pet. 3:7 NIV)

In many cultures, men have been valued more than women, and women have been considered the "weaker partner." But in the life of Jesus, and in some expressions of the early church, women were valued equally to men. For example, Jesus had many female followers. Women were not among those we call the "twelve disciples" because the Twelve were called to represent the 12 tribes of the New Israel, and the 12 tribes of the "old" Israel were all named after men. That does not mean that Jesus valued his female followers less than his male followers.

Jesus seems to have been extraordinarily close to a number of female followers, including: Mary Magdalene, to whom he appeared after the resurrection; the sisters Mary and Martha, who hosted Jesus in their home; and, of course, his mother Mary. All of these women were counted among those in the early church. Many women followed Jesus, were taught by him, and even supported him financially, including Joanna, the wife of Herod's steward Chuza, Susanna, and many others (Luke 8:3). And, it was a group of women who went to the tomb early on Sunday morning and found it empty—the varying accounts of which are told in the Gospels.

In Matthew, the risen Jesus appears to these women and tells them to go tell the disciples. In Mark, the angel in the empty tomb tells the women to go tell the disciples that Jesus has been raised. In Luke, the women go and tell the disciples, but the women's words seem to them "an idle tale" and they do not believe them (24:11). In John, Mary Magdalene runs from the empty tomb to tell Simon Peter and the beloved disciple, "They have taken the Lord out of the tomb, and we do not know where they have laid him" (20:2b).

So, in all four gospels, it is women who are commissioned to be the first evangelists! After meeting the risen Jesus face to face, Mary Magdalene went again to the disciples to announce that she had seen the Lord. Against the expected conventions of the time, the good news of the resurrection was first entrusted to women! Not surprisingly, considering the first-century disparagement of women, the disciples did not believe the women at first.

Women also played a surprising role in the early church, again against the societal norms of the time. Some women were church leaders:

- Phoebe was a deacon of the church at Cenchreae (Rom. 16:1).
- Lydia was the first Christian convert in Europe, and seemingly became the leader of the fledgling church in Philippi (Acts 16:11-15).
- Priscilla and her husband Aquila accompanied Paul near the end of his second missionary journey, and eventually the couple went on their own missionary journeys (Acts 18:18).
- In 1 Corinthians 16:19 we learn that Aquila and Prisca (Priscilla) were leaders of the church that met in their house.

So, women had surprising leadership roles in the early church, in contravention to the role of women at the time and those selected passages that seem to negate the possibility.

Sadly, many churches even today treat women as inferiors. Women cannot serve as pastors in Roman Catholic churches and in most Southern Baptist churches, simply because they are female. Even today certain passages of scripture are used in the subjugation of women.

CONDEMNATION OF DIFFERENT SEXUAL ORIENTATIONS

The Bible has long been used to condemn LGBTQ persons. Perhaps the origin of such condemnation is found in the story in Genesis 19, when the men of Sodom wanted to sexually violate Lot's guests. From that episode was coined the term "sodomy," to connote homosexual relations. Among its many prohibitions, Leviticus details unlawful sexual relations. One prohibition is the command, "Do not have sexual relations with a man as one does with a woman; that is detestable" (Lev. 18:22, NIV). The punishment for such an offense is detailed in Leviticus 20:13, "If a man has sexual relations with a man as one does with a woman, both of them have done what is detestable. They are to be put to death" (NIV). The death sentence is also prescribed in Leviticus 20 for those who curse their father or mother (v. 9) or commit adultery (v. 10), and for a man who has sexual relations with his father's wife (v. 11) or with his daughter-in-law (v. 12).

In the New Testament, "sodomites" are condemned in 1 Corinthians 6:9-10, along with fornicators, idolaters, adulterers, male prostitutes, thieves, the greedy, drunkards, revilers, and robbers. In 1 Timothy 1:9-10, sodomites are included in a list that condemns murderers, fornicators, slave traders, liars, and perjurers. Jude 7 says, "Likewise, Sodom and Gomorrah and the surrounding cities, which in the same manner as they, indulged in sexual immorality and pursued unnatural lust, serve as an example of undergoing a punishment of eternal fire" (NRSV). Romans 1 details God's judgment on ungodliness and wickedness:

Introduction

> For this reason God gave them up to degrading passions. Their women exchanged natural intercourse for unnatural, and in the same way also the men, giving up natural intercourse with women, were consumed with passion for one another. Men committed shameless acts with men and received in their own persons due penalty for their error. And since they did not see fit to acknowledge God, God gave them up to a debased mind and to things that should not be done. They were filled with every kind of wickedness, evil, covetousness, malice. Full of envy, murder, strife, deceit, craftiness, they are gossips, slanderers, God-haters, insolent, haughty, boastful, inventors of evil, rebellious toward parents, foolish, faithless, heartless, ruthless. (vv. 26-31, NRSV)

It would be easy to conclude that such persons are to be condemned. But consider what Paul wrote next in Romans 2:1: "Therefore you have no excuse, whoever you are, when you judge others; for in passing judgment on another you condemn yourself, because you, the judge, are doing the very same things" (NRSV).

Yes, it is possible to find isolated "proof texts" to condemn persons of different sexual orientations. But Jesus never condemned them. He had a heart for persons that the society of his day condemned.

What do all of these "dead end" scripture passages have in common? First, they represent human cultural conditions rather than God's eternal purposes. Second, they represent the human tendency to marginalize and put other people down, whether they be people of another race or another gender or another sexual orientation. Third, they represent elevating certain dead-end passages over other scripture passages that lead to life. The Bible is inspired, but not all the passages of the Bible are of equal value. As Shakespeare wrote in *The Merchant of Venice*, even "the devil can cite Scripture for his purpose."

One purpose of *Spelunking Scripture: The Letters of Paul* is to identify important passages of scripture that lead to life. Pauls' letters convey truth about God's intentions for our lives. But not every word of Paul is of equal value. Some words from his epistles convey the cultural conditions of the time rather than God's purposes. The aim of this book is to explore some important passages from the Epistles that convey God's eternal truth, for example:

- Not Ashamed of the Gospel (Rom. 1:16-17 NIV)
- Sighs Too Deep for Words (Rom. 8:26-28 NRSV)
- Nothing Can Separate Us (Rom. 8:31-32, 35-38 NLT)
- Not Conformed, But Transformed (Rom. 12:1-2 NRSV)
- The Lord's Supper (1 Cor. 11:23-26 NRSV)
- The Love Chapter (1 Cor. 13:4-8, 13 NIV)
- We Do Not Lose Heart (2 Cor. 4:16-18 NRSV)
- All God's Children (Gal. 3:26-28 CEB)
- Christian Freedom (Gal. 5:1, 13-14 CEB)
- Imitate Christ (Phil. 2:5-11 CEB)
- Clothe Yourselves with Love (Col. 3:12-15 NRSV)
- All Scripture Is God-Breathed (2 Tim. 3:16-17 NIV)

Thirteen letters in the New Testament are attributed to Paul. Although some scholars believe some of the letters may have been written, or edited, by Paul's followers, all of the letters begin by identifying Paul as the author. In some letters Paul mentions associates who also send greetings, such as Sosthenes (1 Corinthians), Timothy (2 Corinthians, Philippians, Colossians, 1 and 2 Thessalonians, and Philemon), and Silvanus (1 and 2 Thessalonians). Most of the letters were addressed to specific churches (or groups of churches), although a few were addressed to specific individuals. Probably, most of the letters were intended to be read aloud to assembled congregations, and most were written to address particular needs within the churches. As such, Paul's counsel about certain situations was not meant to be applied universally to all the churches. The passages from Paul's letters identified for this study do have a universal application. Please join me as we explore together these important scripture passages.

NOTES

[1] John A. Broadus, "Memoirs of James Petrigru Boyce," in *Selected Works of John A. Broadus* (Founders Press, 2001) 4:185.

[2] Bob Allen, Baptist News Global, June 23, 2015.

[3] Samuel M. Brooke. *Slavery and the Slaveholder's Religion as Opposed to Christianity* (Cincinnati, OH: 1846), 9.

[4] Tony Cartledge, *Sessions with Genesis* (Macon, GA: Smyth & Helwys, 2012), 8.

CHAPTER 1

NOT ASHAMED OF THE GOSPEL

(Rom. 1:16-17)

For I am not ashamed of the gospel, because it is the power of God that brings salvation to everyone who believes… For in the gospel the righteousness of God is revealed—a righteousness that is by faith from first to last.

(Rom. 1:16-17a NIV)

The first two verses in Paul's letter to the Romans encapsulate the theme of the letter. The gospel, the good news about Jesus Christ, is that God has acted to bring salvation to everyone who believes. Righteousness comes, not through human achievement, but through faith. Paul quotes from Habakkuk 2:4, "the righteous live by their faith" (NRSV). Paul also quotes this Habakkuk passage in Galatians 3:11, alludes to it in Philippians 3:9, and it is quoted in Hebrews 10:38. The point of all those verses is that salvation comes by faith.

Perhaps it would help to read Romans 1:16-17 in some other modern English translations or paraphrases:

> For I am not ashamed of this Good News about Christ. It is the power of God at work, saving everyone who believes—the Jew first and also the Gentile. This Good News tells us how God makes us right in his sight. This is accomplished from start to finish by faith. As the Scriptures say, "It is through faith that a righteous person has life." (NLT)

> I'm not ashamed of the gospel: it is God's own power for salvation to all who have faith in God, to the Jew first and also to the Greek. God's righteousness is being revealed in the gospel, from faithfulness for faith, as it is written, "The righteous person will live by faith." (CEB)

> I am proud of the good news! It is God's powerful way of saving all people who have faith, whether they are Jews or Gentiles. The good news tells how God accepts everyone who has faith, but only those who have faith. It is just as the Scriptures say, "The people God accepts because of their faith will live." (CEV)

> I have complete confidence in the gospel; it is God's power to save all who believe, first the Jews and also the Gentiles. For the gospel reveals how God puts people

right with himself: it is through faith from beginning to end. As the scripture says, "The person who is put right with God through faith shall live." (GNT)

It's news I'm most proud to proclaim, this extraordinary Message of God's powerful plan to rescue everyone who trusts him, starting with Jews and then right on to everyone else! God's way of putting people right shows up in the acts of faith, confirming what Scripture has said all along: "The person in right standing before God by trusting him really lives." (MSG)

I want to preach it because I'm not ashamed of the good news. It is God's power to save everyone who believes. It is meant first for the Jews. It is meant also for the Gentiles. The good news shows God's power to make people right with himself. God's power to be made right with him is given to the person who has faith. It happens by faith from beginning to end. It is written, "The one who is right with God will live by faith." (NIRV)

For I am not *the least bit* embarrassed about the gospel. *I won't shy away from it*, because it is God's power to save every person who believes: first the Jew, and then the non-Jew. You see, in the good news, God's restorative justice is revealed. *And as we will see*, it begins with and ends in faith. As the Scripture declares, "By faith the just will obtain life." (VOICE)

FAITH ALONE
(Rom. 1:16-17)

It was a summer afternoon. We were on the back nine of the East Course at Andrews Air Force Base (now known as Joint Base Andrews). My golfing companions were three Marines, two of whom were members of our church. The afternoon was so hot and muggy that we were sweating before we got to the first tee. We were halfway through our round when, in an instant, the weather dramatically changed. Ominous, dark storm clouds covered the sky.

Suddenly, there was a clap of thunder so loud that it sounded like a cannon. The rain started to fall, just a few drops at first, then a torrent. We pulled our golf carts under some trees to wait out the storm. The rain was falling now in sheets, like a waterfall. Then a bolt of lightning flashed directly over our heads, and another boom of thunder. I said to my friend Pat, who was driving our golf cart, "Let's get the heck out of here," or something to that effect.

The wind was howling, and the rain was coming at us almost horizontally, with some hail mixed in. Pat started driving, across fairways, over hill and dale, through rough and trees, heading for the clubhouse. Visibility was down to about five feet. Somehow, we made it back to the clubhouse, albeit totally drenched, cold, and more than a little shaken. I took off my shoes and poured water out of them. I have been in fierce thunderstorms before, but I have never felt so vulnerable as that day on the golf course. I've developed a healthy respect for lightning and storm clouds ever since.

Martin Luther was a 22-year-old university student, preparing for a career as a lawyer. It was a summer afternoon, July 2, 1505, when he got caught in a violent thunderstorm.

A bolt of lightning struck the ground so close to him that he could feel the hair on the back of his neck standing straight out. Luther was thrown to the ground, terrified for his life. In that moment of crisis, he prayed to St. Anne that if she would save him from the thunderstorm, he would give his life to God and become a monk.

Sure enough, Luther was spared further harm, and he kept his promise. He gave up hopes for a legal career and became a monk. He entered the Augustinian monastery at Erfurt, Germany and studied to become a priest. If ever there were a dedicated monk, it was Martin Luther. He embraced the poverty, chastity, and obedience of the monastic life with ferocious intensity. He wore himself out with prayer and fasting and going to confession. Later he wrote, "If ever a monk got to heaven by his monkery, it was I. If I had kept on any longer, I should have killed myself with vigils, prayers, readings, and other work."[1] But the harder Luther tried to earn his salvation, the more guilty he felt.

Martin Luther had this distorted image of God as an angry judge, rather than as a loving father. Luther lived in fear that God was going to punish him for his sins. He knew he was unworthy of salvation, so he tried ever harder to be good enough to escape eternal damnation. But the harder he tried, the more he worried about the state of his soul.

In 1512 Martin Luther was appointed a professor of theology at the University of Wittenberg. To prepare for his lectures, Luther began to study the Bible, particularly Paul's letter to the Romans. He read Romans over and over again, night and day. It was more than an academic exercise; it was a deeply personal quest. Luther was consumed with the question, What can I do to be saved? The church had given him an answer, but it did not satisfy. The church had told him that salvation comes through the rules and rituals of the church. Going to Mass and confession, paying the tithe, saying all the prescribed prayers, praying to the saints, venerating holy relics, receiving the sacraments—these were the means of salvation, according to the church. Luther did all those things, but still he did not feel forgiven; still he did not feel saved. He even had become a monk and a priest; he had dedicated himself to live a holy life, but none of that was enough.

To Luther's dismay, the church had devised yet another way to offer salvation, and another way to fill the church coffers—the sale of indulgences. Indulgences were thought to be a ticket to heaven—a guarantee of salvation. Indulgences were akin to letters of pardon for the forgiveness of sins: Buy an indulgence and you didn't need to go to confession. Money was all that was required to buy God's forgiveness. Luther was appalled. Such abuse and corruption could not be right. So, Luther was driven to the scriptures, driven to seek to know how sinful man could stand before holy God. And the answer he found in the Bible changed his life, and it changed the church, and it changed history.

How can I be saved? Martin Luther found his answer in Paul's letter to the Romans: by faith alone! This was a radical new idea in Paul's time, and it was a radical idea in Luther's time too. For the Jews, the only way to be right with God was to keep all the commandments. For the Jews, there were 614 specific requirements in the Old Testament law. In addition, there were prescriptions attached to each of these requirements, handed down orally from generation to generation. Only by keeping the law—all the law—could a person hope to be saved. Paul himself had tried to earn his salvation by living a righteous life as a Pharisee. But then Paul was converted to Christ and came to see that salvation comes by faith alone. What we cannot do for ourselves by living righteously, Christ has done for us through his death on the cross.

When Martin Luther read in Romans that salvation comes by faith alone, it was like another thunderbolt had crossed his path. It changed his life forever. No longer was he trapped in that endless cycle of trying to be good enough to deserve God's favor. No longer was he tormented by the guilt of his sins. Now, for the first time in his life, Luther could accept God's forgiveness. He could stop trying to win his way into heaven. He could accept the fact that Christ had died for his sins, and that faith in Christ was all that was required for him to receive eternal life.

Because of Paul, and Martin Luther, and others who followed, we know that salvation comes by faith. Yet even though we know it in our heads, we still can get caught up in the obsession of trying to be perfect. We imagine that if we can just be good enough, God will accept us. But even if we go to church every Sunday, give a tithe of our incomes, pray and read the Bible every day, do acts of charity, and live thoroughly moral lives—none of these is enough to assure our salvation. Only faith can do that. Only faith can give us the courage to stand before Holy God without shame or fear. We don't do good works to *become* Christians. We do good works because we *are* Christians.

Martin Luther did not intend to start the Protestant Reformation. He was only trying to find a way to save his own soul. But the way he found to peace of mind and heart became a pathway for millions of others to follow. Today every Protestant church, every Protestant Christian, owes a debt of gratitude to Martin Luther who taught that salvation comes, not by works, but by faith. And we owe a debt to Paul who wrote in his letter to the Romans that "the righteous will live by faith." To be sure, good works will follow, because the sincere Christian will try to live a moral and productive life. But salvation comes by faith.

LIVE BY FAITH
(Rom. 1:16-17)

More than 500 years ago, Martin Luther, a German priest in the Roman Catholic Church, nailed 95 theses to the door of the church in Wittenberg, Germany. Of course, 500 years ago in Germany, and in the rest of western Europe, the Roman Catholic Church was *the* church. There were no other kinds of churches—no Lutheran churches, no Presbyterian churches, no Anglican churches, no Episcopal churches, no Methodist churches, and certainly no Baptist churches. If you were a Christian, you were a Roman Catholic. If you hoped to be saved, you had to go through the church. You had no other option. The problem is that a church without rivals, a church with absolute power, is subject to corruption. The church in Martin Luther's time had become corrupt.

Luther was especially troubled by the power of the pope. The pope exercised more authority over the church and over the lives of individual Christians than the Bible did. In fact, since the Bible was available only in Latin, and since most people could not read Latin and did not have access to a Bible—even if they could read Latin—most church members did not know what was in the Bible. They had to do as they were told by the pope, the priests, and the other church officials.

Martin Luther was especially troubled by the sale of indulgences. To raise money for building projects and other church funding, the pope had authorized the sale of indulgences for the forgiveness of sins. If you wanted your sins forgiven, or if you wanted forgiveness of sins for people you cared about, then you were encouraged to buy indulgences. It was like the church was selling forgiveness. Luther knew that wasn't right. He was especially persuaded by the book of Romans, and by Romans 1:16-17 in particular. Luther discovered that the Bible does not prescribe the sale of indulgences, but rather teaches that forgiveness and salvation come through faith. Forgiveness and salvation are free gifts of God through faith in Jesus Christ.

In his letter to the Romans, Paul wrote: "For I am not ashamed of the gospel: it is the power of God for salvation to everyone who has faith." Paul said nothing about buying indulgences; salvation comes to everyone who has faith in Jesus Christ.

When Martin Luther read those words in Romans, it was like a light came on in his mind and heart. He became outraged at how the church had perverted the teachings of Paul and other New Testament writings. Luther explained how he came to this new understanding: "At last, by the mercy of God, meditating day and night, I gave heed to the words…'The one who is righteous will live by faith.'"[2] Luther began to understand that salvation is a gift of God through faith. Salvation comes through personal faith in Jesus, not through indulgences or the rituals of the church.

Martin Luther nailed his 95 theses to the church door in Wittenberg to publicize some of the issues he had with the church. Other Christians in other places also had begun to question the authority, teachings, and practices of the Roman Catholic Church. Some "reformers" had been questioning the Church for centuries. But Luther had the advantage of the invention of the printing press, so that his ideas could be more easily disseminated.

Eventually Luther was excommunicated for challenging the authority of the pope. If he not been protected by powerful German nobility, Luther likely would have been arrested and executed for his heretical views. Ironically, Luther's goal was not to start a new church, but to "reform" the established church. It was to be a "reformation" based on faith in Jesus, the authority of the Bible, and the priesthood of all believers.

About 92 years after Martin Luther nailed his 95 theses on the church door in Germany, some religious dissenters in England sought to "reform" the church. The Church of England had broken away from the Roman Catholic Church after Luther did in the 16th century. But some Christians in the 17th century felt the Church of England had not gone far enough. These "reformers" were called "Puritans" and "Separatists."

Whereas Puritans wanted simply to purify the Church of England, Separatists sought to separate from it and form a new church based on the Bible. Some Separatists had read the Bible for themselves and could find no biblical justification for infant baptism. Most of the Reformation churches had rejected the authority of the pope, but they still baptized babies. Radical reformers such as Anabaptists in Europe and Baptists in England and America, rejected infant baptism and thus began practicing believer's baptism. Therefore, the Reformation that Martin Luther had begun in 1517 was taken a step further in 1609 when some of those radical reformers who had been baptized as babies in the Church of England were baptized again as believers on the basis of their personal and voluntary faith in Jesus. Some of those Baptists came to the New World and formed the First Baptist Church of America in Providence, Rhode Island in 1639. Believer's baptism was for them an expression of being saved by faith.

Now, more than 400 years later, Baptists continue to proclaim salvation through faith in Jesus and to practice believer's baptism. We are baptized not to be saved but because we have been saved through our faith in Christ. We are "not ashamed of the gospel because it is the power of God that brings salvation to everyone who believes."

COMING TO FAITH
(Rom. 1:16-17)

What is faith, and how do you get it? Gordon Jackson wanted to know. So, he asked people. He conducted interviews with 210 people of faith—Baptists, Methodists, Lutherans, Presbyterians; men and women; clergy and laypeople. To each one he asked a simple question: How did you come to your faith? He asked, and they told him. The average interview lasted two hours.

Jackson analyzed those interviews and reported the results in a book titled, *Pathways to Faith*. You might think it would be difficult to get people talking about something so personal, but most people enjoyed telling their faith story. One man said, "I've been a Baptist all my life, and no one ever asked me how it was with me and God. Preachers have told me from the pulpit, but no one ever asked me. Thank you for letting me share my faith with you."[3]

Some of Jackson's findings I found to be surprising. For example, he discovered that most people came to their faith gradually. Only 10 percent had a dramatic conversion experience. For the other 90 percent, their faith was an evolutionary process. Some had grown up in the church; others had not. Some had come from a Christian home; others had not been exposed to Christian teachings until they were adults. But for the vast majority, faith did not come like a thunderbolt out of heaven. Most people could not say, "That's when it happened; that was the critical moment." For most of them, faith came over time, as a seed that was planted and gradually grew.

Would you like to guess the number-one influence that led people to their faith? It was not preachers, nor church services, nor reading the Bible, nor watching some religious program on television. It was the influence of caring people. Someone cared about them, and through that caring person or persons, they came to believe that God cared about them too.

In many cases, it was parents or grandparents who played that crucial role in the interviewees' faith development. Especially for children, it is hard to overstate the importance of the climate in the home for laying the foundation for a strong religious faith. When children feel loved and cared for, they develop a basic trust about life, and that basic trust is easily translated into religious faith. But not every child has the advantage of a safe, secure, loving, nurturing home environment. That's where other caring persons come in.

Beyond parents and grandparents, can you guess what other caring persons had a significant impact on the lives of children? I was kind of hoping the interview results would say it was the pastors of their churches. But no, for most of them, the pastors of their childhood did not make that much of an impression. Most of them did not really know their pastors when they were children. The key influencers outside the home were not pastors, but instead Sunday School teachers who communicated care and concern. And what they remembered most was not the lessons their Sunday School teachers taught them. In fact, they could remember little in terms of content. What they remembered most was the kind of persons those teachers were: caring, kind, concerned, and faithful.

For the church to be a community of faith, it must first be a community of caring. People are not interested in how much we believe until they believe how much we care. If we want to share our faith, the way to do that is to communicate genuine love and concern. So, the garden plot for faith is a community of caring. Yet, even within a caring community, how a person comes to faith is still something of a mystery. We can prepare the ground and plant the seed, but it is God who causes faith to grow. It happens in a different way for each individual. God works in each person's life in a way that is unique to that person. If you haven't had a faith experience just like mine, that's okay. We come to believe in God and to accept Jesus in our own ways.

Faith is personal. It is not something we force on or give to another person. We can share our faith with others, but they in their own way make a choice about making faith their own. That is one reason why Baptist churches don't baptize babies. Even though parents want to give their faith to their children, faith is not something you pass on like a family heirloom. Children come to a point in their own lives when they make a faith decision for themselves. The important thing about faith is that it is your own.

I was 11 years old when I decided to be baptized and join the church. I cannot point to an exact moment in time when I became a Christian, because I learned to believe in God and to love Jesus from my earliest years. I was one of those fortunate children who grew up as a Christian, so that I never knew a time when I was not. But even then, at the age of 11, I made a faith decision. As an expression of that faith decision, I walked down the aisle of the church on a Sunday morning during the hymn of invitation and shook the pastor's hand and filled out a membership form. Some weeks later I was baptized as a believer on the basis of my faith in Christ. But I cannot say that I became a Christian in that moment. It was a time when I professed my faith in Christ in a public way.

How does a person come to faith? It is a two-part process. First, it is God reaching out to us in Jesus Christ, offering us forgiveness and salvation and new life. Then, it's our reaching back to God, confessing our need for forgiveness, accepting God's love, and living the new life. As Paul said, we live by faith.

QUESTIONS FOR DISCUSSION/REFLECTION

1. What is faith to you?
2. How did you come to your faith?
3. What persons were instrumental in your faith journey?
4. What is the "righteousness of God"?
5. What does it mean to "live by faith"?

NOTES

[1] *Glimpses*, Christian History Institute, no. 15, 1991.
[2] *Luther's Works*, vol. 34, edited by Lewis Spitz (Muhlenberg Press, 1960), 337.
[3] Gordon Jackson, *Pathways to Faith* (Nashville: Abingdon Press, 1989), 58.

CHAPTER 2

SIGHS TOO DEEP FOR WORDS
(Rom. 8:26-28)

Likewise the Spirit helps us in our weakness; for we do not know how to pray as we ought, but that very Spirit intercedes with sighs too deep for words. And God, who searches the heart, knows what is the mind of the Spirit. We know that all things work together for good for those who love God....

(Rom. 8:26-27a, 28a NRSV)

Sighs too deep for words ... It happened more than 40 years ago. I was fresh out of seminary and serving as associate pastor of a Baptist church in Silver Spring, Maryland. Among my pastoral duties was directing the youth program. One night, after Linda and I had gone to bed, the telephone rang. It was a member of the youth group, and he was so upset he could hardly talk. I managed to understand from him that he was at a local hospital, where his mother had been admitted as a patient. He was asking me to come to the hospital, ASAP. I threw on some clothes, jumped in the car, and got there as soon as I could.

When I arrived at the ward where his mother was a patient, I was met by a nurse with a stunned look on her face. She told me that the patient had died, and that the family wanted to see me. Then she whispered that the patient had died by suicide. Her body was still lying on the bed in her hospital room, and the medical staff could not get the patient's husband to leave the room. I consoled the youth group member who had called me, and then I went into the room to try to console his father.

The man was sitting on the floor, across from where his wife's body was lying. He was weeping softly. I sat down on the floor beside him. I put my hand on his shoulder, but the words would not come. I was praying silently, but I could not pray aloud. What could I say? What could I pray? We simply sat together on the floor, side by side, for a long time. Finally, I stood up, and he stood up, and we left the room together so that the medical staff could come and remove his wife's body. The funeral was held at the church the next week.

I didn't realize it at the time, but later I came to understand that in our weakness the Spirit intercedes for us, with "sighs too deep for words." I certainly did not see in that experience how "all things work together for good," but eventually God was able to bring some good out of that tragic circumstance. It certainly did not compensate for the young man losing his mother, or for the father losing his wife, but over time they and the rest of the family found grace to carry on. As a pastor over the next 40 years, I was present in the aftermath of many other families losing loved ones. Although the pain was real, healing did come. Somehow the Spirit interceded when we did not know how to pray, and somehow God worked for good.

TOO DEEP FOR WORDS
(Rom. 8:26-27)

We were gathered around the dining room table at a bed-and-breakfast in Charleston, South Carolina. There were eight of us on our annual golf trip, which we would take every January. The table was filled with tempting fruits and pastries, and we were all hungry and ready to eat. But then came the awkward moment: Who would say the prayer?

Now, in most situations, when I sit down to eat with a group of church people, the question does not need to be asked. Usually, it is assumed that I will say the prayer. Maybe people think I would be offended if I were not asked to say the blessing, or maybe they think that I am the one best prepared to say grace. Either way, that's okay; it doesn't bother me. I'm used to it. I've been saying public prayers most of my adult life. But this time, it was not assumed that I would be the one to pray.

We were on vacation, and I was not officially "on duty." Besides, there were five ordained deacons among us. Surely, any one of them could say a good prayer. Well, by consensus, Pete Parreco got elected to do it, and he did a fine job. But the whole episode illustrates, I think, a lack of confidence that most of us feel when it comes to prayer. We know we should pray, and most of us do pray, at least in the privacy of our own homes. But if the truth be told, most of us would agree with the scripture that, "we do not know how to pray as we ought."

Prayer, authentic prayer, deeply heartfelt prayer, does not come easily for most of us. We may have a few stock phrases we can use in a pinch. We can pray in generalities. We thank God for our blessings, ask God to forgive our sins, and pray that God will help the less fortunate. But when it comes to more articulate prayer, many of us are at a loss for words. Is there a secret to prayer, we wonder? Are there certain rules to follow, certain tricks of the trade? Is there a proper posture we should assume—standing or sitting or kneeling? Should we bow our heads and close our eyes? Should we place our palms together, or lift our hands toward heaven? What about the words we use? No wonder most of us feel inadequate when it comes to prayer. We have gotten the notion that only if we follow all the rules will our prayers be heard.

Welton Gaddy, in his book, *A Love Affair With God*, says that the first rule of effective prayer is to forget the rules. Gaddy says that many well-intentioned Christians are intimidated by prayer because they are afraid they won't do it right. You can understand why. Many of us grew up in a church environment where the prayers we heard were formal and stilted. There was that unnatural tone of voice that the preacher used when he prayed. Or there was the preacher with the intellectual tone to his prayers. Who were they trying to impress, anyway? Perhaps some of us went to liturgical churches where the prayers were all written out in flowery language. Or, perhaps some of us are unsure how to pray because we had little religious training as we were growing up. Either way, whether we heard many prayers or few, most of us still feel inadequate when it comes to fashioning meaningful prayers ourselves.

There are two basic types of prayer. First, there is public prayer, the kind spoken aloud during a worship service or in a group. By its nature, this type of prayer is more stylized and generalized. When I pray aloud publicly in a group, I am praying for more than just myself. I choose my words carefully because I am seeking to represent the thoughts of many people, and not just my own thoughts. On the other hand, there is private prayer. This prayer is more spontaneous, more personal, sometimes prayed aloud, but more often silently. This type of prayer is more intimate, more specific. The choice of words is not so important as the feeling behind those words.

Many of us are intimidated by the first type of prayer because we are afraid that we will embarrass ourselves if we pray aloud in public. We are afraid that we might stumble over our words, or lose our train of thought, or say something that doesn't make much sense. (I've done all those things, by the way, and lived to tell about it.) But the second type of prayer can be equally intimidating. We can be afraid of private and personal prayer because it requires that we drop all our pretenses and stand before God in naked honesty. This second type of prayer is our focus here.

Public prayer is important, but not all of us are called upon to pray publicly. But all of us do need to pray privately, every day of our lives. I say we "need" to pray because there is a void in our lives without God. Prayer is not so much an obligation as it is a life-support system. I don't have rules for prayer, but I do have some suggestions.

First, be honest when you pray. If you are not honest, you might as well keep silent. God already knows everything about us, so dishonesty is just self-deception. But when we are honest with God, we are honest with ourselves, and this is one way that prayer can help us. If we are honest about our needs, we can begin to understand what is important in life. If we are honest about our sin, we can begin to see where we need to change. If we are honest about our fears and anxieties, we can begin to put things into perspective and gain control of our worries, rather than letting our worries control us. God doesn't care what language we use, or what posture we assume, or what we pray about, as long as we are honest. God wants us to pray in a way that is authentic to who we are. God is big enough to handle our complaints, our doubts, our questions, our cries for help. We don't have to hold anything back when we pray.

Second, be specific when you pray. It doesn't do any good to ask God to forgive your sins unless you are willing to identify what those sins are. It doesn't do any good to ask God to bless others unless you are willing to identify those individuals and think about their needs. When you thank God for all he has done for you, get specific. Remember when God healed you, remember when God delivered you from trouble, remember when God gave you a gift beyond your deserving. We get specific, not because God needs to be reminded, but because we need to be reminded. The fourth-century Christian Augustine prayed to God: "may I know You, may I know myself." That's what specific prayer does: it helps us to know God and to know ourselves.

Third, be persistent when you pray. Don't give up when your prayers are not immediately answered. Keep on praying, even when God seems to be silent. I once heard the

Baptist preacher Carlyle Marney give this advice: When you can't hear God speaking to you, live on the basis of the last clear word you got from God, until you hear another one. In his book, *Contemplative Prayer*, Thomas Merton wrote: "Learn patience in the weary and arid path that takes us through the dry places in prayer." There are times for every person when prayer becomes difficult. Sometimes events in life conspire to push us away from God and to make prayer difficult. Even when the words won't come, turn your thoughts over to God.

In his letter to the Romans, Paul wrote that the Holy Spirit helps us in our weakness when we do not know how to pray as we ought, interceding for us with "sighs too deep for words." When it comes to personal prayer, the words we use, the place we pray, the posture we assume, the time of day, the length of our prayer—all those things—are not that important. What is important is that we pray.

There was a time in my life when prayer would not come for me. It was during my first semester in seminary, and I stopped praying. I started having doubts about God, doubts about the Christian faith, doubts about my most fundamental beliefs. And for a brief time, I gave in to those doubts and stopped praying. My crisis of faith grew so intense that I became ill. One night I awakened at about two in the morning and could not go back to sleep. I knew something was wrong with my body, but I could not figure out what it was. It turned out that I had a liver ailment, and I ended up in the hospital for 11 days. But that night, as I lay on my bed, without even thinking about it, I began to pray. For the first time in months, I began to pray. Looking back on it, I believe the Spirit was interceding for me, with sighs too deep for words.

Maybe you have been like that at some point in your life. Maybe you are somewhere like that now, unable or unwilling to pray. Take heart and don't give up, God's Spirit is present for you too. When we do not know how to pray as we ought, the Spirit intercedes for us in our weakness with sighs too deep for words. Be honest, be specific, be persistent, and the Spirit will carry the deepest prayers of your heart to God.

WHEN THE SKY IS SILENT
(Rom. 8:28)

It was a Saturday morning in February of 2003. A festive crowd had gathered at the Kennedy Space Center in Cape Canaveral, Florida. Officials from NASA, the families of the astronauts, local politicians, and even representatives from the Israeli government were there to welcome back the triumphant crew of the space shuttle *Columbia* from their successful 16-day mission. Everyone in the crowd was buzzing with excitement and anticipation, all the while listening for the tell-tale sonic boom that would herald the return of the orbiter. But that morning the sky over Cape Canaveral was strangely silent.

Meanwhile, the sky over Texas was resounding with a cacophony of sounds. There was a thunderous clap, then a series of booms as the space shuttle broke apart some 200,000 feet above the earth. The seven brave astronauts aboard the *Columbia* never had a chance. Back in Florida, family members were hastily herded into buses and ferried to a secluded part of the Kennedy Center compound. There would be no sound from the sky over Florida that morning, and no joyous return, for the shuttle was lost and everyone in the crew had perished.

This was the second disaster in America's space shuttle program. It brought back memories of the *Challenger* explosion 17 years before. When something such as this happens, our first question is "why." Why did it happen? What went wrong? What caused such a catastrophe to take place? It is a human impulse to want to know why when bad things happen.

Sometimes our search for answers turns theological: "Where was God in all of this? Why did God allow this to happen?" It is one of the "Big Eight" objections to Christianity identified by journalist Lee Strobel in his book, *The Case for Faith*. Strobel named eight barriers to belief, eight objections to the Christian faith that have troubled many people. And the first question, the first objection is this: "Since Evil and Suffering Exist, A Loving God Cannot." Strobel quotes theologian John Stott: "The fact of suffering undoubtedly constitutes the single greatest challenge to the Christian faith. Its distribution and degree appear to be entirely random and therefore unfair. Sensitive spirits ask if it can possibly be reconciled with God's justice and love."[1]

When Strobel, a former legal editor for the *Chicago Tribune*, began to do research for his book, he traveled to Toronto, Canada to interview a writer named Charles Templeton. Years ago, Templeton had been a close associate of the evangelist Billy Graham. Templeton had first met Graham in 1945 at a Youth for Christ rally. They later were roommates and colleagues on a preaching tour of Europe, alternating in the pulpit as they preached evangelistic rallies. Still later, Templeton founded a church and preached to overflow congregations in its 1,200-seat sanctuary. Yet, despite his success as an evangelist and pastor, doubts began to gnaw at him, intellectual objections to the validity of the Christian faith.

Charles Templeton and his friend Billy Graham began to privately debate the truth of scripture and the claims of Christianity. For his part, Graham searched the Bible for answers, prayed, and finally reached a point where he said, "I'm going to allow faith to go beyond my intellectual questions and doubts." Templeton went the other way and allowed his doubts to overwhelm his faith. He resigned from his church, left the ministry, and moved back to Canada where he became a commentator and novelist.

When Lee Strobel interviewed Charles Templeton years later, Strobel asked him, "Was there one particular thing that caused you to lose your faith in God?" Templeton answered, "It was a photograph in *Life* magazine. It was a picture of a black woman in northern Africa. They were experiencing a devastating drought. And she was holding her dead baby in her arms and looking up to heaven with the most forlorn expression. I looked at it and thought, 'Is it possible to believe that there is a loving or caring Creator when all this woman needed was rain?' How could a loving God do this to that woman?"[2]

Herein lies one of the toughest objections to the Christian faith: How could a loving God allow such undeserved pain and suffering in the world? We can understand when people suffer from their own bad judgment and foolish decisions and sinful actions. Such suffering is the result of natural and logical consequences. But as John Stott said, the distribution and degree of suffering in the world appears to be random and therefore patently unfair. People do not necessarily suffer in direct proportion to their own deserving. Some people seem to suffer far more than they deserve. It is the seemingly undeserved pain and suffering in the world that is the greatest challenge to a loving God. When a woman from drought-stricken Africa looks up to heaven with a starved baby in her arms, and the sky is silent, what then? How can we reconcile our belief in a loving and caring God with so much pain?

This question has perplexed humanity from ancient days. The book of Job in the Old Testament is essentially a dramatic narrative that wrestles with the question but provides no easy answers. Theologians call it the question of theodicy, reconciling the justice and love of God with the existence of evil and suffering in the world. The Bible deals with suffering in various ways. In some cases, the Bible teaches that suffering is the result of sin. Sometimes we suffer as a result of our own sins. Other times we suffer as a result of the sins or mistakes of others. The Bible also views some suffering as the result of living in a fallen world.

This world is not a perfect paradise, not the garden of Eden. We live in an imperfect and fallen world, and some suffering is a result of that condition. In a perfect world there would be no disease, no natural disasters, no suffering of any kind. But we do not live in a perfect world. So, according to the Bible, some suffering is simply a condition of the kind of world in which we live.

The Bible also deals with suffering as a mystery, as the book of Job concludes. Suffering is a mystery beyond our human ability to comprehend or fully understand. So, some suffering is our own fault or the fault of others; some suffering is the result of living in a fallen, imperfect world; and some suffering is simply a mystery beyond our ability to comprehend or fully understand.

But there is another biblical perspective on suffering that is reflected in Paul's letter to the Romans: Suffering can be redeemed. In other words, God can bring good out of suffering. God can transform suffering into something redemptive. A positive result or transformation does not automatically happen, however. Suffering can cause people to lose hope, as it did for Charles Templeton. The difference is faith. For the person of faith, suffering is not the final word. For the person of faith, the final word is God and the faith that God can use suffering to bring about good. In Romans 8:28 Paul wrote, "in all things God works for the good of those who love him" (NIV). It is not that suffering automatically leads to something good, but that God works in all things—even suffering—to bring good out of them. It is God, and our faith in God, that can transcend the bad things in life for some higher purpose and good.

The *Columbia* disaster was a tragic loss for our nation and for the families of the astronauts, but there are other losses that affect us even more personally. If you live long enough, you will suffer loss. My cousin, Julie, who was just a year older than I, died from a brain tumor at age 52. When anyone dies an untimely death, we ask "why." Why did God take her at such a relatively young age? There are no easy answers. Suffering is more often a mystery. But God works in all circumstances to bring good out of mystery.

When Julie was first diagnosed with a brain tumor, she had surgery and chemotherapy and radiation and every other available treatment. The cancer went into remission, and we all hoped and prayed that she was cured. It was a difficult time for Julie and for her family, but God used that experience to draw Julie closer to him. She became more active in her church, and she developed a depth of character and faith that sometimes only comes from suffering. So, even in that, God was working to redeem her suffering into a greater good. We miss her, but we don't worry about her. And we give thanks for the faith journey that led her all the way home. "All things work together for good for those who love God." When the sky is silent, the difference is faith.

ALL THINGS WORK TOGETHER FOR GOOD
(Rom. 8:26-28)

January is not my favorite month. Some bad things have happened in my life in January.

I served as pastor of Village Baptist Church in Bowie, Maryland for 33 years. On January 8, 2000, the church building burned. That might seem like a long time ago, but for those of us who were there, we will never forget it. It was one of the most traumatic events of our lives. It wasn't as traumatic as the death of a family member or a friend, but it was very painful. Not only did we lose the church building, but we also found ourselves in exile, with no place to call our own. We didn't just lose material things. We lost our sense of place, our sense of having a home.

For two Sundays after the fire, the congregation met at the Pointer Ridge Fire Station in Bowie. Then, for 34 months after that, we met at Bowie Alliance Church. Neither of those places felt like home. A physician in the community rented us office space, but that didn't feel like home either. So, it was not a good experience after the church burned. For me, it was a miserable experience. Not only did we lose the building, but during the time of our displacement we also lost a lot of members. I'm glad I didn't know at the time that was going to happen, but I did know it was going to be a struggle.

Yet, as soon as the fire was out, as we were standing in the parking lot watching the smoke rising to the sky, a passage of scripture came to mind. Somehow, I knew God was going to bring good out of it. In fact, Romans 8:28 became the theme verse for what we were going through after the fire. For a time, I would print Romans 8:28 at the bottom of every piece of correspondence I sent, "All things work together for good for those who love God."

Now, saying all things work together for good does not mean all things are good. Having a church building destroyed by fire is not good. Getting a brain tumor is not good. Losing a loved one is not good. But God is at work in all circumstances, even in negative circumstances, to bring good out of them. Do you see the distinction? God is not the cause of all the bad things that happen to us. Many things that happen grieve God too. Yet, God is at work in those bad things to bring good out of them.

January 8, 2000 was one of the worst days of my life, the day the church building burned. There was another bad day for me in January, many years before that. On January 20, 1974, I became seriously ill. I had just completed my first semester at seminary. I was enrolled in the "J-term" before the second semester. J-terms were optional courses that crammed an entire semester's course into one month—January, June, or July. My seminary had a partnership with other seminaries in the region. Students had the option of taking a course at a partner seminary just to get the experience of another theological tradition.

In the January 1974 J-term, I was taking a course on the writings of the German theologian, Dietrich Bonhoeffer, at the Louisville Presbyterian Theological Seminary. About midway through the J-term, I got sick. I ended up in the hospital for 11 days. Fortunately, I was able to withdraw from the class on Bonhoeffer, so I did not get a failing grade in the course.

The initial diagnosis of my illness was "something like" hepatitis, but the doctors never really pinned down what was wrong with me. I now believe it was a liver ailment related to a medication I had been taking that had been prescribed by a dermatologist. I came to find out that one of the possible side effects of that medication was liver damage. In any case, January 20, 1974 was the beginning of one of the worst times in my life.

After spending 11 days at Baptist Hospital in Louisville, I had to drop out of seminary. I had enrolled for the spring semester, but I was too tired and too weak to go to class. I had no choice but to return to my parents' house in Fort Worth, Texas to recuperate. Hepatitis and other liver diseases are difficult to treat. There are medications available now, but the main treatment back then was bed rest and dietary restrictions. I felt lousy day after day, for months. I had little energy or appetite. It made me sick at my stomach to try to read for any length of time, because it was a strain to focus my eyes. Basically, I was homebound for months, with nothing to do. Needless to say, I became depressed.

When you are 22 years old and have to drop out of school and can't work, and you feel lousy every day and are back home living with your parents and have no social life and don't know when you will ever be able to get on with your life—you get depressed. It was a desperate feeling. In no way would I call that experience a good thing. I was miserable for months, and I didn't feel completely well for another five years. Yet, looking back on that experience now, I can see that some good did come out of it. I believe that God was at work even in that negative circumstance to bring about good.

In fact, several good things came out of that bad thing. First, my experience of serious illness gave me an empathy for people in pain. I'm not sure I could have gained that empathy any other way. I know what it's like to be sick, to be in the hospital, to wonder if you will ever get well. I know what it's like to feel lousy day after day. I know what it's like to feel useless and helpless. And that knowledge, based on personal experience, gave me an understanding of what other people are going through. It helped me to be a better pastor. I learned lessons from being sick that I never could have learned sitting in a classroom at the seminary. Looking back, I can say that God was at work in my illness to bring good out of it. Now, I wouldn't wish sickness on anyone. I pray that I will never have to endure that kind of illness again. But I became a more empathetic and compassionate person through it.

Another good came out of that bad experience. Had I not gotten sick and had to drop out of seminary for a semester, it is unlikely that I would have ever met Linda, my future wife. Because I had to miss a semester, I was not able to graduate when most of my classmates did. The spring semester of my third year in seminary was not my last semester. Most of my friends were getting ready to graduate, but I had another semester to go. I was bummed out about that. To deal with my sadness, I accepted an invitation to participate in a drama at a church that one of my friends attended. I never would have gone to that church otherwise. I had my own church, and that church was in another part of town. But at that other church, while taking part in the drama, I met Linda. God used that experience of illness for good.

God used the experience of the church burning for good. Had the church building not burned on January 8, 2000, the congregation would not have become the church we became. Not only did we eventually have a bigger and better building than we had before the fire, but we also became a larger and more diverse congregation. But it didn't happen automatically. Rebuilding was not easy.

As I said, during the 34 months of our displacement, our congregation grew smaller. About a third of the people who were with us before the fire were not around when we moved back into the rebuilt building. That was terribly discouraging. But something good came out of something bad. God used that experience to make Village Baptist Church a more welcoming congregation. Gradually, new members started joining the church and enriching the fellowship.

Another good that came out of the fire is that I don't take as many things for granted. After we rebuilt, I thanked God every day that I could come to the new building, because there were three years when we didn't have a building. Also, I promised God after we moved back into the rebuilt church that we would use the building to the maximum to serve people. Not only would the building serve our congregation, but it also would serve the community.

Many community groups began to benefit from using the building: Girl Scouts, two AA groups, three CDA (Chemically Dependent Anonymous) groups. Several times a year the Music Teachers Association of Bowie would hold recitals or keyboard exams in the sanctuary. The church began to serve as a polling place for primary and general elections. Then the church became a temporary homeless shelter for one week each winter for the Warm Nights ministry of Prince George's County. Village Baptist Church could not have hosted Warm Nights in the old building. So, though the fire that destroyed the original building was not good, God brought good out of it.

"All things work together for good for those who love God." No matter what you are going through in your life right now, remember: God is working to bring good out of it. That's what kept me going when I got sick on January 20, 1974. That's what kept me going when the church building burned on January 8, 2000. Romans 8:28 became a theme verse for my life. Now, January is still not my favorite month, mainly because it's too cold to play golf. But God can still bring good out of January, or any month, or any experience of life.

I once heard a preacher say, "It's not what you're going through; it's what you're going to." When you're going through tough times, sometimes all you can do is hold on, in the faith that God is holding on to you. Sometimes all you can do is believe in the promise that God will lead you to a better day.

Sometimes life gets so hard that we don't even know how to pray. But the Spirit helps us in our weakness and intercedes for us with sighs too deep for words. And God, who searches our hearts, and knows us better than we know ourselves, will give us the grace to carry on.

NOTES

[1] John Stott, quoted by Lee Strobel in *The Case for Faith* (Zondervan, 2000), 33.
[2] Ibid., 39.

QUESTIONS FOR DISCUSSION/REFLECTION

1. What does the phrase "sighs too deep for words" mean to you?
2. Why do we not know how to pray as we ought?
3. How does the Spirit help us in our weakness?
4. How has the Spirit interceded for you?
5. How has God worked together for good in your life?

CHAPTER 3

NOTHING CAN SEPARATE US
(Rom. 8:28-39)

> *I am convinced that nothing can ever separate us from God's love. Neither death nor life, neither angels nor demons, neither our fears for today nor our worries about tomorrow—not even the powers of hell can separate us from God's love.*
> (Rom. 8:37-38 NLT)

The apostle Paul did not have an easy life. In 2 Corinthians 11:23-28, he detailed some of his hardships: five times he received 39 lashes; three times he was beaten with rods; once he was stoned; three times he was shipwrecked; once for a night and a day he was adrift at sea. On frequent journeys he was in danger from rivers, from bandits, from Jews, from Gentiles, in the city, in the wilderness, at sea, and from false brothers and sisters. "In toil and hardship, through many a sleepless night," Paul was "hungry and thirsty, often without food, cold and naked" (v. 27). Besides all that, Paul was under daily pressure because of his anxiety for all the churches.

For Paul, and for most Christians in the first century, life was not easy. Life was difficult and dangerous. Yet, because nothing can separate us from God's love, difficulty and danger are not the final words. Because nothing can separate us from God's love, life in Christ can be victorious too. As Paul wrote, "even the powers of hell can't keep God's love away" (Rom. 8:38, NLT).

EUCATASTROPHE
(Rom. 8:28-39)

The past can have a powerful pull on us. I'm talking about negative events from the past. You get burned once, and you don't want to get burned again. Something bad happens to you, and you're careful to try to avoid the same kind of situation again.

Some years ago, a terrible train wreck happened just north of Baltimore. It was a catastrophe. A passenger train slammed into some Conrail locomotives that were on the wrong track. Many people were killed, and many more were injured. Finally, after repairs were made and the track was reopened, service was restored. Some television news crews went to Union Station in Washington, D.C. to see if anyone would dare to ride on the passenger train that was going north through Baltimore. There were a good number of people who got on board. But they all went to the back of the train; the first two cars were completely empty. On a rational level, the passengers knew it was perfectly safe. But on a gut level, they figured they had better play it safe—just in case.

The past can exert a profound influence on us, but perhaps we give the past more power over our lives than it is due. Sometimes I wonder if we don't become hostages to irrational fears, so that our lives are filled with unnecessary worries and anxieties and concerns.

A child is raised in a fraught home environment. The father is an alcoholic. The mother suffers from depression. The child endures physical and emotional abuse. When the child grows up, the scars remain. Those negative childhood experiences have left their mark. This adult child doesn't trust other people and lacks the ability to admit mistakes or express tenderness or love. The tragedies of the past are repeated over and over again.

A child grows up in a nice home where love is seldom expressed. There is pressure to behave, to conform, to do well in school. The child does not measure up to expectations, the parents express disapproval, and ultimately the child rebels. The child squanders his potential. He gives up. He adopts a defeatist attitude toward life. "I can never measure up," he says, "so why try?" The past hangs around his neck like a heavy weight.

A marriage breaks up. Maybe it was his fault; maybe it was hers. Who knows? Now there is an emotional toll to be paid. There are feelings of rejection, worthlessness, and failure. There is the temptation never to love again, for loving creates vulnerability, and vulnerability creates the potential for more pain.

A loved one dies. We are overwhelmed with grief. We cannot imagine going on without that person. Life gets about as dark as a cloudy sky at midnight. We wonder, "Can I ever be happy again? Can I ever be hopeful again? Can I ever find meaning in life again?"

There are countless other possible personal catastrophes I could mention. Most of us have been through negative life experiences. A tough childhood, trouble at home and/or school, love-related troubles, health problems, work problems, the death of a family member—most of us have had things happen to us that caused great pain. And those negative events do not disappear just because they are in the past. We remember what happened, and that memory shapes our expectations of the future. If it happened once, it could happen again, our insides tell us. Our pessimism becomes a self-fulfilling prophecy. We give up in relationships because we might be harmed by love again. We stop trying to better ourselves because we probably couldn't do it anyway.

Who was it who said, "Those who do not learn from the mistakes of the past are doomed to repeating them"? There is danger in not learning from the past, but there is also the danger of over-learning from the past. Failures, disappointments, and hurts can teach us too well. When these negatives are all we have learned, we are doomed to repeat them.

It is to this situation that we hear a new word from Romans 8. But instead of repeating the verses, I want to summarize this powerful message with one word: "eucatastrophe." Coined by the novelist, J.R.R. Tolkien, he was talking about the opposite of catastrophe. He was referring to a catastrophe for good, a positive upheaval, a reversal of events that would become a blessing instead of a curse.

This is where the message of the Bible comes in. According to the Bible, Jesus Christ is our eucatastrophe—the good catastrophe, the positive upheaval, the great unexpected blessing from God. This is Paul's message in Romans 8.

Paul presents a realistic picture of life. Yes, bad things do happen. In verse 35 Paul lists a litany of negative experiences: trouble, calamity, persecution, hunger, cold, danger, even the threat of death. No question about it, there is much potential in our world for hurt. Some of us have had, or will have, catastrophes happen to us. But catastrophes need not have the final word. Just because something bad happened to us does not mean that we are doomed to re-run the tragedies of the past.

The biblical view of history is not cyclical. Rather, it is linear. We are not just going around in circles, but instead moving toward a goal. The future does not have to be a re-hash of the past. Into the future can break something new, something unexpected, something good.

Romans 8 teaches us that Jesus Christ is the eucatastrophe of human history, the good catastrophe, the positive upheaval, the harbinger of blessing instead of curse. Jesus Christ means that God is for us, that God is with us, that God will never leave us or desert us. In every circumstance, God is present to turn things around, or at least, to turn us around. This is the new word that breaks the cycle of history, that interrupts our predictions of doom and gloom, that lifts before our hearts the promise of hope. Jesus Christ means eucatastrophe. Jesus Christ means you can be free from the past. Jesus Christ means God is in your future, and God is more powerful than anything that has happened or will happen to you again.

The movie, *Children of a Lesser God*, is based on a stage play of the same name. It is the story of two people, a deaf woman and a teacher for the deaf, who struggle to find some common ground of meeting. As the story unfolds, we learn that the deaf woman has been terribly hurt in the past. As she was growing up, she was often the subject of ridicule by other children. At one point in her life, she tried to learn to speak, but some people made such fun of her that she felt humiliated, and she vowed never to try to speak again. Her parents did not know what to do with her, so they sent her away to live at a school for the deaf. As a teenager, starved for affection, she would occasionally come home on weekends. Her older sister, who could hear, had lots of boyfriends, and this deaf girl longed to be like her "normal" sister. But what boy would want a deaf girl?

Finally, out of desperate loneliness, she discovered that she could get attention from boys if she would yield to them sexually. The word got around, and soon she had plenty of boys interested in her. But they were only using her. None of them really cared about her, and she knew it. Not one of them would even take her out for a Coke. They would only take her to a dark place and get what they wanted. As a result, this lonely deaf girl grew up to be an angry young woman, filled with rage and hatred and contempt for others and herself.

Then, unexpectedly, a new teacher came to the school where this young woman now worked as a janitor. This teacher was not put off by her anger and hostility. Instead, he began to try to get to know her as a person. She rejected him at first, but he would not give up. He looked through all the anger and bitterness on the outside to see a person of value, potential, and beauty on the inside. He came to understand how she had been hurt by cruel people and tragic events of the past. He knew that she had every right to be filled with rage at the injustice of it all—the injustice of being born deaf, the injustice of parents who didn't love her enough, the injustice of boys who used her for their own pleasure and then threw her away like a piece of garbage. He felt anger and rage too. But the teacher somehow saw beyond the past and looked to the future. He believed in what the young deaf woman could become. And gradually, tenderly, his love began to wear down her defenses. Gradually, tenderly, they found a place to meet between her silence and his sound.

This is a story of eucatastrophe, of positive upheaval, of grace. And in a profound sense, it is our story too, for we can feel like "children of a lesser God." Sometimes the negative events of the past make us angry or bitter or fearful or closed off to new possibilities. But One has come to us who loves us. One has come to us, a Teacher yes, but so much more. One has come to us who sees something beautiful in us, beneath the rough and rugged surface of our lives. One has come to us who can transform the past into a future full of hope. One has come to us whose name means eucatastrophe. And when we place our faith in him, when we follow him, only God knows what blessings this One will bring.

MASTER OF MY FATE
(Rom. 8:28, 31-39)

We met for the first time at the National Children's Medical Center in Washington, D.C. He was the nephew of a member of our church, and the step-grandson of a former church member. I had heard about him, but we had never met face-to-face. He lived out of state with his mother and stepfather, but he had come to National Children's Medical Center because his condition had gotten worse. I did not know how much worse until I arrived at the hospital shortly after lunchtime.

The doors to the pediatric ICU were open, so I just wandered in. There, in the first room on the right were his mother and stepfather, and Danil. I could tell things were not going well. His mother had climbed into the hospital bed with Danil, her lanky 6'4" 16-year-old son. She had her arms around him to comfort him, as best she could. Danil was struggling to breathe, despite having a breathing apparatus strapped to his face to force oxygen into his lungs. I spent the next three hours at Danil's bedside, or in the family consultation room just outside the ICU, talking with Danil and with his parents and his grandmother. It was an intense, and heart-wrenching, and yet deeply moving experience.

While his parents were meeting with the doctors to make decisions about Danil's treatment, his grandmother and I stayed by his bed so Danil would not be alone. It was obvious that his grandmother had spent many hours caring for Danil. She knew where to get ice chips and juice, how to shift around the pillows to make him more comfortable, what all the numbers on his monitors meant that measured his respiration rate and blood pressure and heartbeat. I was meeting Danil for the first time, but it didn't take long for me to feel as though I knew him.

Danil was a bright young man, with a surprising grasp of the English language, and an amazing will to live. He had been born in Russia, but he had moved to the U.S. after his mother had married his stepfather. He asked me to pull up a stool and to sit by his bed so we could get better acquainted. After some time talking about his condition, Danil said to me, "Now, tell me about yourself." In all my years of visiting people in the hospital, I don't recall anyone ever asking me to tell them about myself. But that's the kind of person Danil was, always thinking of others. When Danil heard a baby crying in another room, his heart was filled with compassion. "Poor baby," Danil said. As sick as he was, Danil did not think just about himself.

In response to Danil's request, I told him I was his uncle's pastor and his grandmother's former pastor. Yes, Danil remembered his uncle and his aunt and his cousin, their daughter who was about his age. Danil perked up when he talked about his cousin. I could tell he had a special interest in her. Then I asked Danil about his other interests. He said he played basketball, liked swimming, and hoped to go back to school one day. When he had first come to the U.S. just four months earlier, he had attended school for two weeks. Then he got so sick he had to go to the hospital. Since then, Danil had been in two hospitals, and in the ICU three times. He had received two series of radiation treatments and three rounds of chemotherapy, but the cancer was too widespread.

Danil clutched a small, blue-covered Russian New Testament in his large, teenage hand. He tightly held onto that Bible as if it were a lifeline, and I suppose, in a profound sense, it was. Some missionaries to Russia had given Danil that Russian New Testament, and he had begun to read it for himself. He had finished the gospel of Matthew and was beginning to read the other gospels, but now he was too sick to read anything. All he could do was clutch that small Bible to his heart and think about the One whose story it told.

Danil knew about Jesus. He had seen the *Jesus* video in Russian several times during those few days that he had been back at home. It was obvious that Danil thought about Jesus a lot. Danil told me that he had prayed for Jesus to heal him. I knew from talking with his grandmother that Danil had also prayed for the other children in the ICU to be healed. Danil wore a bronze cross on a chain about his neck. When the technician came in to take an x-ray, his grandmother removed the chain with the cross from around Danil's neck. But after the x-ray was over, Danil wanted to wear the cross again.

As the afternoon wore on, Danil continued to labor to breathe. A few times he had to cough up some blood. There was little anyone could do except to try to make him a little more comfortable. After meeting with his parents in another room, the doctor came in to talk with Danil. The doctor asked his grandmother and me to leave. Danil now knew that his prognosis was not good, that he was going to die and probably soon. How does a 16-year-old boy find the courage to face death? I can only believe it came from Danil's faith. Danil had written a date in the back of his Russian New Testament—May 1, 2001. It was the date he had accepted Jesus Christ as his Savior and Lord. Danil had prayed for Jesus to cure him. But even if Danil would not receive the miracle he had prayed for, Danil still had faith.

Later that afternoon, while the doctors and nurses inserted a tube down Danil's throat to help him breathe, his grandmother and parents and I gathered in the small consultation room. A pastor from the African nation of Cameroon was there, along with one of his parishioners whose infant daughter was in the hospital. The African pastor shared his own testimony of how God had answered his prayer and begun to heal the infant daughter of the lady in his church. He said he believed in the power of God to do miracles. He asked us if we wanted him to pray for Danil.

We could not go into Danil's room while the medical staff was performing the procedure on him, so the six of us joined hands there in the consultation room and prayed. I prayed aloud first, then the pastor from Africa prayed. As he prayed in French, the woman whose daughter was sick translated into English. Danil's mother, who spoke Russian and only a little English and no French, prayed with her own thoughts. Together we prayed for Danil, that if it were God's will, he would be healed, but that in any case God would be with him. The miracle of healing did not come. But God was with Danil. Danil died about 10:30 p.m. that night, but he was never alone. I will never forget Danil's courage and his faith.

One week before Danil was told he was going to die, another young man knew he was going to die, but the circumstances could hardly have been more different. Timothy McVeigh was sentenced to die for the worst act of domestic terrorism in American history. The bomb he detonated outside the Federal Building in Oklahoma killed 168 innocent men, women, and children. McVeigh approached his death without any hint of apology or remorse. In one last defiant act, he copied a poem in his own handwriting to serve as his final statement. The poem was "Invictus," from the 19th-century British poet William Ernest Henley.

> Out of the night that covers me,
> Black as the Pit from pole to pole,
> I thank whatever gods maybe
> For my unconquerable soul.
>
> In the fell clutch of circumstance
> I have not winced or cried aloud,
> Under the bludgeonings of chance
> My head is bloody, but unbowed.
>
> Beyond this place of wrath and tears
> Looms but the horror of the shade,
> And yet the menace of the years
> Finds, and shall find me, unafraid.
>
> It matters not how straight the gate,
> How charged with punishments the scroll,
> I am the master of my fate:
> I am the captain of my soul.

The poet Henley never dreamed that his poem would be used to try to justify the warped immorality of a mass murderer like Timothy McVeigh. In his poem, Henley was expressing his convictions about the hurts and setbacks he had experienced in his own life. At the age of 12, he had developed tubercular arthritis. In his teens his left foot had to be amputated. He had other health problems later in his life, and he wrote "Invictus," which is Latin for "unconquered," while once again in the hospital. For Henley, "Invictus" was an expression of courage in the face of difficulties, certainly not a justification to commit terrorism.

Timothy McVeigh was not the master of his fate. He was executed by the very government he sought to destroy. And standing before the judgment seat of God, McVeigh is certainly not the captain of his soul.

Danil, though half his age, understood what Timothy McVeigh did not. Danil understood that the master of our fate, the captain of our souls, is not ourselves, but God. We are all in God's hands. Ultimately, God is in control. The good news of the gospel is this: Nothing can separate us from the love of God through Christ Jesus our Lord.

The funeral service for Danil was held the Friday after he died. I would not pretend that Danil's death was easy, for him, or for those who loved him. It was an excruciating experience for all of us. But I know that even in that awful circumstance, God was there, just as God was with Danil. Now we know Danil is at home and at peace with his Father in heaven.

Who can separate us from the love of God? Nothing, if we place our faith in God's Son, Jesus Christ. I thank God for Danil's faith and for the new life he now lives in God's presence. I'll never forget a young man named Danil and how God used him as an instrument of his unconquerable love.

SWINGING IN THE RAIN
(Rom. 8:31-39)

My friend Jere Allen is one of the most positive people I have ever known. Some people might remember him as Dr. Jere Allen, former executive director/minister of the D.C. Baptist Convention. But I know him in another context. Jere and I played golf just about every Thursday with other Baptist minister friends. For many years Jere has gone on golf trips that I have organized to Alabama, Ocean City, Maryland, North Carolina, South Carolina, Mississippi, and other places. So, I've spent a lot of time with Jere playing golf and traveling to play golf.

Some years ago we were together on a golf trip to Myrtle Beach, South Carolina. Among our group were Mark Miles and his sons Jeremy and Gary, and my son Marc. We arrived in Myrtle Beach mid-morning on a Monday, and our intent was to play golf that afternoon, but it was pouring rain. We stopped for lunch, hoping the rain would stop. It didn't. By the time we got to the course where we had reserved a tee time, the course was closed. There was standing water everywhere. Jere was not to be deterred. He suggested we try to find a golf course that was open. We called around, and sure enough we found a place to play further south. Never mind that the course was soggy, and never mind that the sky opened on us near the end of our round. Jere said it was just about the best golf course he had ever played.

The next day, Tuesday, it rained again. We played anyway—two rounds, morning and afternoon. At each venue, Jere said it was just about the best golf course he had ever played. Wednesday it rained again. We played anyway. I think there was one other group on the entire course when we started. It was raining so hard the Miles boys went back to the condo to play cards, but Jere Allen and Marc Salmon and I played in the downpour. And we played a second round in the afternoon on another course in the rain. Thursday, more rain, but we played anyway. That afternoon we went out for a second round on another course. (If you're keeping score, that's seven rounds of golf in four days, all in the rain.)

Just as we were about to begin our afternoon round, I noticed the sky getting dark to the west. I pointed out the darkening sky to Jere, and he ran to the car to get his rain suit. By the time we reached the first tee, the sky was almost black. Then the rain started falling, harder and harder. Jere took a couple of practice swings with the rain pelting down on him. By the time he hit his drive, the rain was coming down in sheets. The wind was blowing the raindrops almost sideways. It was raining so hard that none of us could see where his tee shot landed. Mark Miles said, "I'm not playing in this," so he turned his golf cart around and headed for the club house. I said, "I'm with Mark." Jere reluctantly followed. By the time we got back to the clubhouse it was a deluge. After about an hour's rain delay, we were back out on the golf course, splashing down the fairway on every hole.

Our last day, Friday, you guessed it—it rained again. We played golf five straight days in the rain! On the way to the airport Friday afternoon Jere exclaimed, "We were really fortunate with the weather this week!" "Fortunate?" I replied. "It rained every single day!" "Yeah," Jere said, "but we still got to play!" For Jere Allen, the glass is always half full, not half empty. He can see the sunny side of almost any situation. He is one of the most positive, hopeful, upbeat, enthusiastic, optimistic people I know.

The apostle Paul was a positive person too. His hopeful, upbeat, enthusiastic, optimistic attitude comes through in almost every letter he wrote. And it wasn't because life was easy for Paul. His life was exceedingly hard. Just about everywhere he went as a Christian missionary he had trouble. His preaching about Jesus stirred up fierce opposition. During the course of his missionary journeys he was criticized, maligned, mistreated, persecuted, beaten, stoned, thrown into jail numerous times, shipwrecked, deprived, hungry, thirsty, sick, and in trouble (2 Cor. 11:24-28).

On top of all that, Paul had a "thorn in the flesh"—some nagging physical problem or chronic infirmity that vexed him continuously. Yet Paul could say, "I have learned to be content." With regard to that thorn in the flesh, he wrote: "Three times I appealed to the Lord about this, that it would leave me, but he said to me, 'My grace is sufficient for you, for power is made perfect in weakness'" (2 Cor. 12:8-9). In verse 10 Paul added, "Therefore I am content with weaknesses, insults, hardships, persecutions, and calamities for the sake of Christ; for whenever I am weak, then I am strong."

In another of his letters, Paul wrote:, "I have learned to be content with whatever I have. I know what it is to have little, and I know what it is to have plenty. In any and all circumstances I have learned the secret of being well-fed and of going hungry, of having plenty and of being in need" (Phil. 4:11-12). In verse 13 Paul revealed the secret of his contentment: "I can do all things through him who strengthens me."

At the end of chapter 8 in his letter to the Romans, Paul laid out the secret to contentment even further: It's all a matter of faith. Paul had an indomitable spirit, not because of what he had done, but because of what God had done in Jesus Christ. Paul could give thanks in every circumstance, not because of the circumstances themselves, but because of a reality greater than the circumstances, namely the grace and the generosity and the love of God. Paul, who sang in chains in a jail cell, was almost singing when he wrote to the Romans, "If God is for us, who is against us? He who did not withhold his own Son, but gave him up for all of us, will he not with him also give us everything else?"

Paul went on to ask, "Who will separate us from the love of Christ? Will hardship, or distress, or persecution, or famine, or nakedness, or peril, or sword?" These were not rhetorical questions. They were reflections of Paul's own life. He had experienced hardship, distress, persecution, famine, nakedness, peril, and sword. But through it all, he had been sustained, strengthened, and filled with courage and peace by the love of Christ.

Most of us have not had to endure all that Paul faced, but we have our own struggles. And in all the struggles of life, a positive attitude is a powerful force for good. The Bible calls this positive, hopeful, optimistic attitude "faith." We do not fight the battles of life alone. God is with us. God is on our side. As Paul said, "If God is for us, who is against us?" This does not mean that every battle will be won, nor that every illness will be healed and every obstacle overcome. But it does mean that "nothing can separate us from the love of God in Christ Jesus our Lord."

Some years ago, when Jere Allen preached in my church, he shared with the congregation about his battle with cancer. Jere was going into the hospital the following week for surgery. Our church prayed for him and his recovery. Jere did have surgery, and he did recover, and he resumed his active lifestyle of playing golf and distance running.

To celebrate his 65th birthday, Jere trained and ran in a marathon, a footrace of more than 26 miles. Then, to prove it wasn't a fluke, he completed the Marine Corps Marathon two years later at age 67. Then, at age 71, he ran in the Peachtree 10K race in Atlanta, as he had done many times before. Jere told me he trained harder for that race than he ever had. As it turned out, perhaps he overdid it. He began running the race faster than he ever had, much faster than his target time. At the 4.5-mile mark, his legs buckled, and he fell face-first onto the pavement. He skinned his hands and his knees and opened a gash on his forehead. He was bleeding so profusely that he had to stop and receive medical attention. But Jere refused to quit the race. After about 10 minutes, he got up and continued running until he had reached the finish line. He was battered and bruised and bleeding, but he finished the race. He even had to get stitches in his forehead after the race was over. But he never gave up.

Paul said, "In all these things we are more than conquerors through him who loved us." That does not mean we will win every race, or even that we will finish. But it means that through our faith in Christ, we can face the challenges of life with a victorious spirit. Maybe you need some encouragement in your own race of faith right now. Remember: absolutely nothing can separate us from the love of God in Christ Jesus our Lord.

QUESTIONS FOR DISCUSSION/ REFLECTION

1. In what ways is God for us?
2. What challenges do you face in your life that God can help you overcome?
3. What is the "overwhelming victory" that is ours through Christ?
4. What are your fears for today or worries for tomorrow?
5. Can anything ever separate us from Christ's love?

CHAPTER 4

NOT CONFORMED, BUT TRANSFORMED
(Rom. 12:1-2)

Do not be conformed to this world, but be transformed by the renewing of your minds, so that you may discern what is the will of God—what is good and acceptable and perfect.
(Rom. 12:2 NRSV)

How do we discern what is the will of God? Paul said we are to present our bodies as a living sacrifice to God, as contrasted with the dead animal sacrifices of other religions. A living sacrifice means we dedicate ourselves to God. Rather than conforming with the cultural conditions of the world around us, we are transformed by the renewing of our minds. This transformation enables us to discern what is good and acceptable and perfect. We become transformed into new persons by allowing God to change the ways we think and act. No longer following the customs and behavior and mindset of the prevailing culture, we discover a new culture based on the way God wants us to live.

Discerning the will of God is possible as we follow Jesus and as we learn from exploring important passages of scripture. We also learn from each other as we study the Bible together and as we see examples of Christian living. Throughout his letters, Paul assumed that the Christian life would be lived in community with other believers, not in isolation. That is why he addressed his readers as "brothers and sisters" and as "one body in Christ" (v. 4).

TRANSFORMED, NOT CONFORMED
(Rom 12:1-2)

Believe it or not, I got my driver's license when I was 14 years old! I grew up in Texas, and back then a lot of young people worked on farms or ranches. It was not uncommon for even young teenagers to drive a tractor or some other farm equipment. So, driving a car or a truck at age 14 did not sound as crazy then as it does today. By the way, shortly after I got my driver's license, the law was changed to make 16 the minimum age for driving a car or truck.

When I got my driver's license in 1965, the hottest car out there was the Ford Mustang. It had just come out the year before, and was popular from the beginning. So, after I got my driver's license, I wanted a Mustang. The problem was, I did not have enough money to buy a Mustang. Most of my money came from mowing lawns, and from the laundry and dry-cleaning plant where I worked after school and on Saturdays, earning the princely sum of 75 cents an hour. Mustangs were selling for about $2,500 in

1965, so it would take a lot of hours at the laundry to be able to afford one. But I never gave up hope. In my wildest of teenage dreams, I imagined that my parents were going to give me a new car.

The reason I imagined that my parents were going to give me a new car was because the year before, the Christmas of 1964, my parents had given my grandmother a new car. It was a surprise gift, and I was almost as excited as she was. Well, if it happened once, I figured, it could happen again. So, the following year, I was looking under the Christmas tree for a small box with my name on it containing a set of car keys. It wasn't there. But I kept on believing. When Christmas of 1966 came, I was sure my parents were going to give me a Mustang. It didn't happen. But in the summer of 1967, I was given a car—not a new Mustang, but a used 1960 Renault. The car had belonged to my brother-in-law, and he and my sister gave it to me.

The 1960 Renault was a far cry from a new Mustang. It was an import from France, and back then, most imports were not made very well. The VW Beetle was the exception, but this was a French Renault, not a German Volkswagen. The car was basically a tin can on wheels, with a squirrel cage motor in the back. The paint was cracked and faded; one of the windows wouldn't roll up all the way; the top speed was about 45 miles an hour. There was even a place in the floorboard that had rusted through so that I could see the pavement beneath me. But it was a car, and I was happy to have it.

I was happy to have it, that is, until other people started to share their opinions about my car. The manager at the laundry where I worked laughed when I showed him the engine in the back of my 1960 Renault. He said it looked like a sewing machine motor. That took me down a notch. But what did he know? Then I drove my Renault to high school. Some of the kids in the parking lot laughed at it. They said it looked like a Fred Flintstone car. That wasn't funny to me. No teenager likes being laughed at by other teenagers. If I had been driving a new Mustang, no one would have been laughing at me. But I wasn't driving a new Mustang. I was driving a joke of a car that, at first, I was happy to have, but now I was embarrassed to be seen in it.

Peer pressure can be a powerful influence on anyone. We want other people to like us, not laugh at us. We want to fit in, not stick out. We want to be respected, not ridiculed. And sometimes in our efforts to get others to like us and to fit in and to be respected, we go along with others' expectations and standards and values rather than following our own way of living. It's not easy to be a Christian in a culture where many people don't seem to care anything about God, and a lot of people don't go to church, and some people are even hostile toward religion.

Paul understood what it was like to live in a non-Christian culture. The Christians in Rome were surrounded by people who did not share their beliefs. If you think our culture is self-centered and materialistic and obsessed with sex and violence, ancient Rome was even worse. The vast majority of people did not go to church, and if they had any religious beliefs at all, they certainly didn't believe in Jesus or in the one true God. If it's not easy to be a Christian today, imagine how difficult it was for Christians living in ancient Rome.

Not Conformed, But Transformed

So, Paul wrote a letter to the tiny minority of Christians in Rome to encourage them to remain true to their beliefs and lifestyle, despite overwhelming peer pressure to abandon their faith. When Paul wrote, "present your bodies as a living sacrifice," he was saying, "worship God by the way you live." It would have been easy for the Roman Christians to sacrifice an animal on an altar, and then go out and live as everyone else did. But that's not what God wanted.

God wants Christians to present our bodies as a living sacrifice, to live in a way that is holy and acceptable to God. This means we don't just go along with what everyone else is doing. So what if they laugh at us? We've got to be true to ourselves, and true to our faith in God.

Paul continued, "Do not be conformed to this world, but be transformed by the renewing of your minds, so that you may discern what is the will of God." The key to living a Christian life is to be transformed, not conformed. The Greek word for transformed is *metamorphoo*, from which we get our English word, "metamorphosis." It means a change from one form into another, a transformation. As a caterpillar is transformed into a butterfly, we as Christians are transformed from a self-centered way of life into one that is centered around God. And that God-centered life is evident by the way we live. We live, not according to the expectations of others, but according to an internal standard that comes from our relationship with God.

I read some years ago that Warren Buffett's net worth was estimated at $45 billion. (He is worth much more than that now.) Buffett made most of his money through shrewd investments, by following his own sense of direction rather than by listening to the opinions of others. I found it interesting that Warren Buffett does not live like a billionaire. Rather than living in a mansion, he resides in a modest house in Omaha, Nebraska. He doesn't ride in a chauffeured limo, but drives himself around town in a nice car—and nothing ostentatious. The one luxury Buffett allows for himself is a private jet for air travel. Other than that, he estimated at the time that his personal living expenses were not more than $150,000 a year. Perhaps the most amazing thing about Warren Buffett is that he promised in 2006 to give away 99 percent of his personal fortune, most of it going to the Bill and Melinda Gates Foundation.[1]

What drives a guy like Warren Buffett? He lives by what he calls "the inner scorecard." Rather than living the way most other rich people live, Buffett has a different way to measure success. He acts according to his own conscience, rather than to other people's expectations of him. Warren Buffett still wants to be successful financially, but his goal in making money is not just to make his own life better. He wants to make other people's lives better too.

Buffett admits he wasn't always so philanthropically minded. When he started out in business, all he wanted to do was make a lot of money. But his first wife, who died in 2004, was a big influence on him. She was largely responsible for a deep transformation in her husband. She operated by an "inner scorecard" too. An ardent supporter of civil rights, she was involved in helping to integrate Omaha in the 1960s. She went so far as to represent blacks who wanted to buy houses in white neighborhoods. She took Warren to hear people such as Martin Luther King Jr. speak. Buffett recalls a line in one of Dr. King's speeches:

"It may be true that the law can't change the heart, but it can restrain the heartless." Buffett began to think deeply about what he could do to work for a more just society.

As Christians, we operate by an inner scorecard, a different way of measuring success. Our inner scorecard is the mind of Christ. It's not that we don't care about the opinions of others. It's just that we care about God's opinion more. Living by the will of God should be the greatest ambition of our lives. We find our greatest fulfillment when we live in harmony with the one who made us. This fulfillment comes not from being conformed to the world, but from being transformed by the spirit of Christ.

By the way, I finally did get a Ford Mustang. I kept working at the laundry and dry cleaners and saving my money. Then in 1968, during my senior year in high school, I finally bought the car I had wanted: a blue Ford Mustang. It was my pride and joy. My sister sold the old Renault for about $90. But you know, as much as I wanted that Mustang, and as hard as I had worked and saved to buy it, eventually I sold it and bought another car. I discovered that even a Ford Mustang is not the ultimate goal in life. Knowing and doing God's will is the ultimate goal in life. Be transformed, not conformed, and what you want and what you have will be the same.

COUNTERCULTURAL CHRISTIANITY
(Rom. 12:1-2)

My wife Linda and I attended the wedding of our friend Jim Holladay in Louisville, Kentucky. It was the most unusual wedding we have ever seen. It was more like a worship service than a wedding. For example, the congregation sang four hymns. How many weddings have you been to where you sang even one hymn, much less four? The wedding was held in the Baptist church where Jim serves as pastor. Jim's brother, who is also a Baptist minister, officiated. There were scripture readings from the Old Testament and the New Testament and the Apocrypha. We all stood when the gospel lesson was read. There were several prayers, including a prayer of confession printed in the bulletin, along with responsive readings and a congregational affirmation of faith.

Instead of wearing a tuxedo, Jim wore a business suit. Instead of wearing a white wedding dress, his bride wore a very attractive lady's business suit. There were no attendants—no best man or maid of honor. There were no flower girls or ring bearers or ushers. There was no wedding march, no "Here Comes the Bride." During the first hymn, Jim escorted his mother to the front, seated her in the second row, then took his seat on the first pew. Jim's bride, Ruth, escorted her mother to the front, seated her in the second row, then sat next to Jim on the first pew. Jim's older daughter and Ruth's sister each did readings. Ruth's nieces sang a trio, a hymn from the hymnbook. Jim's younger daughter played the violin.

When it came time for exchanging vows and rings, Jim and Ruth took their place on the platform. Jim's brother asked for an affirmation from the members of both families. The family members responded in unison: "We give our blessing and promise our loving support." After Jim and Ruth were pronounced husband and wife, they exited the sanctuary while the congregation sang a recessional hymn.

Not Conformed, But Transformed

The wedding was not traditional, but it was very appropriate for Jim and Ruth. Jim is a pastor (Ruth calls him a "professional Christian"), and Ruth is the daughter of missionaries. She grew up in Liberia, Africa, so traditional American wedding customs have little meaning for her. This was her first marriage, and Jim's second. Neither Ruth nor Jim felt the need to conform to the usual wedding customs. They created a ceremony that was meaningful for them. They wanted it to be more like a church service than a wedding. It was an act of worship.

There was something countercultural about Jim and Ruth's wedding. They didn't even want wedding gifts (although we sent them one anyway). Marrying later in life, they didn't feel compelled to adhere to traditional rituals. They got married on their own terms. And they did their best to make their wedding as "Christian" as possible. They didn't want the focus to be on them, but rather on God. And they wanted to place their wedding in the context of God's goodness and grace.

I first heard the word "countercultural" back in the 1960s. It is a sociological term used to describe the values and behaviors of any group that runs counter to the mainstream culture of the day. In the 1960s, countercultural young people began to question the values and norms of their parents and grandparents. There was great countercultural upheaval, particularly opposition to racial segregation and the Vietnam War. Other values came into question, such as the role of women and sexual mores. Many countercultural figures arose in the 1960s: Muhammad Ali, Martin Luther King Jr., the Beetles, Ralph Nader, and others. Each in their own way challenged the prevailing values and norms of the time. This countercultural movement led to a revolution in terms of race relations and women's rights. It challenged racial segregation, the war in Vietnam, and gender inequality.

Jesus was a countercultural figure of his day, and Christianity was a countercultural movement. The Christian era ushered in a whole new set of values, norms, and behaviors that changed society for the good. In the second century an anonymous Christian author wrote a letter to a high-ranking pagan official. Known as *The Epistle to Diognetus*, this treatise sought to explain how Christians differed from the dominant culture of the day. Here is an excerpt from this second-century epistle.

> Christians are not distinguished from others by nationality or language or customs. For they neither inhabit cities of their own, nor employ a particular form of speech, nor lead an eccentric lifestyle. While they live in Greek as well as barbarian cities…, and follow local customs in dress, food, and the rest of their ordinary conduct, they display to us their wonderful and confessedly striking method of life.
>
> They marry like others and beget children, but do not expose their offspring. They share their meals, but not their wives. They are in the flesh, but do not live after the flesh. They pass their days on earth, but are citizens of heaven. They obey the established laws, but surpass them in their private lives. They love all people, but are persecuted by all. They are slandered, yet vindicated. They are reviled, yet

bless. They are insulted, yet repay the insult with honor. They do good, yet are punished as evil-doers.

In a word, what the soul is in the body, Christians are in the world. The soul dwells in the body, yet is not of the body, so Christians dwell in the world, yet are not of the world.[2]

In his letter to the Romans, Paul wrote: "Do not be conformed to this world, but be transformed by the renewing of your minds, so that you may discern what is the will of God—what is good and acceptable and perfect."

This is the challenge of Christian living: not to be conformed to this world, but to be transformed by the Spirit of God renewing our minds. We are transformed, so that we may discern what is the will of God. As *The Epistle to Diognetus* stated, Christians are not distinguished by their nationality or language or customs or form of speech or eccentric lifestyle. Rather, Christians are distinguished by "their wonderful and confessedly striking method of life." In other words, Christians are distinguished by their countercultural values, behavior, and way of life.

The challenge of Christian living is to be in the world but not of the world. Of course, our lives will reflect some of the culture around us. But when it comes to what is important to us, to what we value and do, Christians seek to reflect the teachings of Jesus and not the prevailing customs of mainstream culture.

When Linda and I were in Louisville for Jim and Ruth's wedding, I saw a story on the front page of the local newspaper that caught my eye. The story was about a church in Louisville that was planning an "open carry church service." In other words, the church leaders were encouraging people to wear handguns to church! An advertisement for the service stated: "We are asking responsible handgun owners to attend this service, openly wearing their sidearm." The pastor of the church is a gun enthusiast, as are many of his parishioners. So, they came up with the idea to invite people to wear their handguns in holsters as an expression of their Second Amendment rights. They were even going to raffle off a handgun, and representatives from various gun shops and firing ranges were going to be there to show their products and promote gun safety.

As I read about this "open carry church service," I asked myself whether this church was promoting the values of culture or the values of Christ. I know there are many responsible gun owners, but I do question the judgment of church leaders who encourage people to bring weapons to a worship service.

There is an old saying, "When in Rome, do as the Romans do." Paul had a different message. He wrote to those in Rome to do as Christ would do. When Paul said, "present your bodies as a living sacrifice," he was saying to let all that you do be an offering to God.

A SERIOUS CALL TO A DEVOUT AND HOLY LIFE
(Rom. 12:1-2)

Every Saturday I turn to the back of the METRO section of *The Washington Post* and read the church ads, giving attention to the sermon titles for Sunday. Some of the titles are boring, but others are intriguing. A title such as "A Serious Call to a Devout and

Holy Life" would not entice much interest: it's boring. "Serious," "devout," and "holy" are good words, but in a church ad they would not be inviting to most people in our contemporary society.

The sermon title I just referenced comes from a book written almost 300 years ago by an Anglican minister in England named William Law. His book, *A Serious Call to a Devout and Holy Life*, is a classic of Christian devotional literature. It's still available in print, or you can download the digital version of the text for free. I recommend it, but I must warn you it was written in the language and the style of three centuries ago. It's not easy reading.

William Law wrote the book because he was concerned about the level of personal spirituality among the people of his day. He noticed there was a disconnect between people going to church and the way they lived the rest of their lives. People acted religious on Sunday when they went to church services, but the rest of the week they acted like everyone else: their lives were anything but devout and holy. So, William Law wrote the book to try to encourage people to take their Christian faith more seriously; to inspire the Christians of his day to be more devout and holy in their daily living. The title of the book may sound antiquated, but the theme could hardly be more relevant.

Paul had a similar concern for the people of his day. He wrote a letter to the church in Rome, in part to encourage the Roman Christians to be faithful in their daily Christian living. Paul was writing to people whose surrounding culture was anything but Christian. Rome was the most important city of the ancient world, politically, economically, and culturally—similar to Washington, D.C. today. It was the capital city of the Roman Empire, filled with important people with important work to do. But it was a thoroughly pagan city.

The culture was polytheistic and amoral. Religious life in Rome featured the worship of Greek and Roman gods and rites and rituals from all manner of cults and mystery religions. Slavery was a dominant institution, and the Coliseum with its gladiator games was a major source of entertainment. Women were treated as inferiors in all strata of society, and prostitution was an accepted form of social behavior. Given that pagan culture, it was not easy to be a Christian in Rome.

Paul knew the challenges the Romans faced. That's why he wrote in Romans 12:1, "I appeal to you brothers and sisters by the mercies of God to present your bodies as a living sacrifice, holy and acceptable to God, which is your spiritual worship."

Paul was alluding to sacrifice as an act of worship. It was an image familiar to most people in the ancient world, as many ancient religions used sacrifice as a worship ritual. Even the Jews offered sacrifices of animals or agricultural produce to give thanks to God and to atone for their sins. Other religions offered sacrifices to appease the gods or to seek divine intervention or help. In contrast, the early Christians did not sacrifice animals or agricultural produce in their worship services. Instead, they interpreted the death of Jesus on the cross as the ultimate and final sacrifice for sins, a sacrifice so complete that any other sacrifice would be futile and meaningless. Instead of offering a sacrifice on an altar, the early Christians observed the Lord's Supper, which they used to remember the sacrificial death of Jesus on the cross.

In a sense, Communion became the sacrifice of the early Christians. That is why the Communion Table was sometimes called an altar: the elements of the bread and the wine represented the body and the blood of Jesus sacrificed on the cross. But the Lord's Supper did not represent the sacrifice they made to atone for sin. Rather, the elements of the Lord's Supper represented the sacrifice that God made through his son Jesus Christ.

Paul was not calling for a return to animal or agricultural sacrifice as a part of Christian worship. Rather, in his letter to the Romans, using sacrificial imagery, Paul said to let your bodies be a living sacrifice to God—which is your spiritual worship. In other words, let your sacrifice to God be holy and acceptable living. Paul didn't say to present your souls as a living sacrifice to God, but rather your bodies should be a living sacrifice. This means that all we are and all we do should be dedicated to God—not just what we do in church on Sunday mornings, but the totality of our lives is to be given to God. Every moment of our lives, every thought we think, every word we speak, every action we take—these we do out of our love and gratitude and commitment to God. Worship is not just what we do in church on Sunday mornings; it is what we do with all of our lives. We present our bodies as a living sacrifice to God.

These days, a popular way of saying "all the time" is 24/7. Some people are on call 24/7 in their jobs, available 24 hours a day and 7 days a week. As a pastor, I was on call 24/7. Every so often I would get an emergency phone call in the middle of the night or on my day off or while I was away on vacation. I didn't mind getting those calls if they were emergencies. Being a pastor is a 24/7 deal. Being a Christian is also a 24/7 deal. It is not limited to Sunday mornings at church. We are "on duty" as Christians every hour and every day of our lives. We are to live distinctively Christian lives wherever we go and whatever we do.

Paul wrote in Romans 12:2, "Do not be conformed to this world, but be transformed by the renewing of your minds." It's easy to be conformed to this world, to buy into the customs and values of our culture. The problem is that sometimes our secular culture is opposed to the values of the Christian life. We live in a culture whose credo seems to be "anything goes, as long as you can get away with it."

As Christians, we are called to live by a higher set of values. We are not to be conformed to the values of this world, but we are to be transformed by the renewing of our minds. As Christians, we don't live by the letter of the law, but by the Spirit of Christ, who lives in our hearts. This is what transforms our lives by the renewing of our minds, the Spirit of Christ that lives within us. When our lives are transformed by the renewing of our minds, doing the right thing becomes second nature to us. In every situation where we are confronted with a moral choice, we choose to live for Christ, because Christ lives in us. Our highest value, our number-one priority, is not ourselves, but God.

"A Serious Call to a Devout and Holy Life"—not many of us would describe our lives as devout and holy. We shy away from a "holier than thou" attitude. We are aware of our failures, shortcomings, and sins. God is holy; we are not. But Christ calls us to devout and holy living, to a renewing of our minds and a transformation of our lifestyles. Christ calls us to worship him, not with some animal sacrifice on an altar, but with the living sacrifice of our lives. Our natural tendency is to go along with the crowd, when in

Not Conformed, But Transformed

Rome to do as the Romans do. But Christ calls us to something better and higher than the ways of the world. Christ calls us to be like him. Conformed or transformed: Which will it be?

QUESTIONS FOR DISCUSSION REFLECTION

1. What does it mean to present our bodies as a living sacrifice?
2. How is "spiritual worship" different from what we do on Sunday mornings in church?
3. In what ways are we "conformed to this world"?
4. What does it mean to be transformed by the renewing of our minds?
5. What is the will of God for your life?

Notes

[1] Rana Foroohar, "Warren Buffett Is on a Radical Track," *Time*, January 23, 2012.
[2] *Timeless Witness: Classic Christian Literature Through the Ages*, edited by A.N.S. Lane (Hendrickson Publishers, 2005), 27-28.

CHAPTER 5

THE LORD'S SUPPER
(1 Cor. 11:17-28)

This is my body that is for you. Do this in remembrance of me. This cup is the new covenant in my blood. Do this, as often as you drink it, in remembrance of me.
(1 Cor. 11:24b, 25b NRSV)

We call it the Lord's Supper, or Communion, or the Eucharist. It is one of the most important rituals of the Christian church. The institution of the ritual at the Last Supper is recounted in Matthew 26:26-29, Mark 14:22-25, and Luke 22:19-20. In all three versions, Jesus gives bread and the cup to his disciples, and he interprets these elements as symbolizing his body and blood, in anticipation of his coming death. He instructs them to repeat the ritual, "in remembrance of me." In John's version of the Last Supper, Jesus dips a piece of bread into the dish and gives it to Judas, but there is no "Lord's Supper," per se, in John's gospel.

In 1 Corinthians 11:20 Paul calls the ritual "the Lord's supper," as he addresses the abuses of communal meals among the believers in Corinth. Rather than sharing the meal equitably and in a spirit of Christian love, some were eating before the others arrived, some were getting drunk, and others were going hungry. Such abuses made a travesty of what the Lord's Supper was intended to be. Paul instructed the Corinthian Christians to wait for one another before beginning to eat. If they were too hungry to wait, they should eat at home before they came together.

Although the ritual of the Lord's Supper often took place in the context of a common meal, known as love feasts (Jude 12) or the agape, the words of institution in 1 Corinthians 11:23-26 came to be used as a ritual of worship, whether or not it was connected with a communal meal.

In our time, the Lord's Supper is commonly observed as a part of corporate worship, and only occasionally connected with a common meal. Some churches observe the Eucharist daily; others observe Communion weekly or monthly and/or on special occasions such as Maundy Thursday or New Year's Eve Watchnight services. Paul did not tell the Corinthians how often they should share the bread and the cup. He only provided guidance for how to do it when they did. Many worship leaders continue to use these words of institution that Paul received from the Lord and handed on to the Corinthians, and to subsequent readers of his letter.

EXAMINE YOURSELVES
(1 Cor. 11:23-28)

The Lord's Supper is intended to unite Christians. Instead, too often it has become a ritual that divides. More than 45 years ago, when I was attending seminary, I spent one month as an exchange student at the Roman Catholic Saint Meinrad Monastery, College, and Seminary in southern Indiana. It was a rich experience. I lived in the dormitory and ate in the dining hall with the Catholic seminary students. Many evenings after class I went to the on-campus tavern, not to drink, since Baptist seminary students were supposed to abstain from alcohol, but to socialize with the Catholic students and even some seminary professors who had no prohibitions against raising a glass or two.

I went to Mass every day, either in the small seminary chapel or in the large parish church connected to the monastery. In almost every instance I was warmly welcomed and invited to take part in everything that took place…except for the Eucharist, or as we call it, Communion. When it came time during the Mass for worshippers to process to the altar to receive the bread and the wine from the priest, I was not allowed to participate. I was told that since I was a Baptist, and since Baptists have a different understanding of the Eucharist than Roman Catholics, I was not eligible to receive Communion. Some of my Catholic friends even apologized that I was excluded, but it wasn't their decision. It was a matter of church doctrine, and in the Catholic Church, doctrinal matters are not open to interpretation—the rules come down from above.

It is true: Baptists (and most other Protestants) and Catholics do understand the Lord's Supper differently. For Baptists, the bread and the cup are symbols of the body and blood of Christ. For Catholics, the bread and the wine are the body and blood of Christ. For Baptists, the Lord's Supper is an ordinance, a symbolic ritual of remembrance. For Catholics, the Eucharist is a sacrament that conveys God's grace through the elements of the bread and the wine. Also, most Baptists substitute grape juice for wine, whereas Catholics would be aghast if there were anything but wine in the chalice. In addition, Baptists serve each other Communion, whereas the elements in the Catholic Eucharist can only be distributed by the priest or other approved church officials.

So, there are some substantial differences in the way that Baptists and Catholics interpret and practice Communion. And because of those differences, I was not allowed to take Communion in the Catholic Church when I was a student at the Catholic seminary, and I am still not allowed to take Communion in any Catholic church today. Catholics practice "closed Communion," meaning it is closed to all outside their faith.

Sometimes even Catholics are precluded from taking Communion. I heard about a Catholic woman who was denied the Eucharist by the priest during her mother's funeral. It happened in Gaithersburg, Maryland. When the woman approached the altar to receive Communion, the priest placed his hand over the bowl containing the bread. The priest told the grieving daughter, "I cannot give you Communion because you live with a woman, and in the eyes of the church, that is a sin." Apparently right before the funeral began, the priest learned that the woman had a female partner. To add to the woman's distress, the priest left the altar while she was delivering her mother's eulogy, and he refused to go to the cemetery for the graveside committal. When the woman asked where the priest was, she was told that he had suddenly taken ill.

After the account of what had happened hit the media, the Archdiocese of Washington issued this statement—documented by many news and online sources—indicating that the priest had not followed accepted procedure:

> When questions arise about whether or not an individual should present themselves for communion, it is not the policy of the Archdiocese of Washington to publicly reprimand the person. Any issues regarding the suitability of an individual to receive communion should be addressed by the priest with that person in a private, pastoral setting.

The priest was later suspended from his position, not for refusing to give Communion to the woman, but for intimidating other members of the church staff.

Who is eligible to receive Communion? Only those who are without sin? If that were the case, then none of us would qualify. Paul wrote to the believers at Corinth about the way they practiced Communion. After explaining how the Lord's Supper was instituted by Jesus, Paul wrote, "Whoever, therefore, eats the bread or drinks the cup of the Lord in an unworthy manner will be answerable for the body and blood of the Lord. Examine yourselves, and only then eat of the bread and drink of the cup" (1 Cor. 11:27-28). But what does it mean to eat the bread and drink the cup "in an unworthy manner"? Does it mean that some Christians should be excluded from taking Communion?

To understand what Paul was saying, we need to understand the larger context of this passage. Paul had heard reports about abuses that were going on in the Corinthian church, including divisions among the congregation. Factions had arisen in the church, perhaps along social or economic lines. Typically, in the church in Corinth the Lord's Supper would be shared at the end of a common meal, sometimes called an agape feast. But Paul heard that some church members were eating before others had arrived, leaving some in the congregation to go hungry. Thus, the poorer members of the church were humiliated by the more affluent members who arrived earlier and ate all the food. Even worse, some church members were getting drunk during the meal, thereby making a mockery of the Lord's Supper.

Obviously, Paul was upset when he heard about these abuses and divisions within the church. So, he wrote that they should not take the Lord's Supper in an "unworthy manner," meaning, they should be considerate and respectful of one another and remember what the Lord's Supper represents. That's why Paul wrote, "Examine yourselves, and only then eat of the bread and drink of the cup."

I have heard this passage interpreted to mean that some Christians are unworthy to receive the Lord's Supper and that therefore the priest or the pastor or the deacons or some other authority should deny it to them. That is not what I interpret this passage to mean. The truth is that none of us is without sin. When Jesus shared the Lord's Supper with his disciples on the night before he died, none of them were without sin. Jesus knew that one of them was going to betray him, and one of them was going to deny him, and all of them were going to desert him. But Jesus gave them the bread and the cup anyway. Being without sin is not a prerequisite for receiving the Lord's Supper. The truth is that none of us is worthy, yet Christ invites us to receive from his table anyway.

As a pastor, every Communion Sunday when I would give the invitation to the Lord's Supper I would say, "This table of the Lord is open to all fellow Christians. Although no one should partake of these sacred emblems impenitent or without faith in Christ, we invite all who are sincerely seeking him to receive from his table." I did not take those words directly from the Bible, but they are a concise statement of who is invited to take Communion. Basically, we leave it up to the individual to decide. As Paul said to the Corinthians, "Examine yourselves, and only then eat of the bread and drink of the cup."

In my church we practiced "open Communion," meaning the Lord's Supper is open to all Christians, not just Baptists, and not just members of that church. We are all sinners in need of God's forgiveness, mercy, and grace. Obviously, we should not take Communion "impenitent," or without an attitude of repentance. If we say we have no sin and have no need to repent, then the Lord's Supper is meaningless to us. Likewise, if we have no faith in Christ, then the Supper is meaningless. That's why no one should partake impenitent or without faith in Christ. So, those are the criteria—a penitent spirit and faith in Christ.

What about children? Should children take Communion? If a child has been baptized as a believer, of course! There is no age limit to the Lord's Supper. Some churches encourage children to take Communion. The United Methodist Church, for example, says that even young children may receive Communion. The United Methodist Book of Worship provides this direction: "All who intend to lead a Christian life, together with their children, are invited to receive the bread and cup." Some churches, such as Roman Catholic, have a set age when children begin to take Communion, usually at age 6 or 7. First Communion is a big deal in those churches. Some churches say a child should be confirmed before taking Communion, usually at age 11 or 12 or 13. The traditional Baptist practice has been to wait until after a child has been baptized as a believer to take Communion.

Personally, I would follow Paul's advice and say, "examine yourselves." I would leave it up to the parents to determine when it is appropriate for their child to take Communion. The Bible does not specify that baptism is a prerequisite for Communion. When Jesus gave the Lord's Supper to his disciples on the night before he died, none of them at that point had been baptized "in the name of the Father, and the Son, and the Holy Spirit." Believer's baptism, as we know it, came after Pentecost, after the followers of Jesus received the Holy Spirit.

If parents determine that their child has faith in Jesus and understands what Communion means, I have no problem with a child taking the Lord's Supper. Conversely, if parents believe it would be better for a child to wait until after making a profession of faith in Christ and being baptized, I certainly support that decision too. Obviously, a child who does not yet have faith in Jesus and does not yet understand what it means should not take Communion. But parents should decide until children are old enough to decide for themselves.

The Lord's Supper

The Lord's Supper was intended to unite believers in Jesus, not divide them. It is a ritual of remembrance that welcomes sinners, not condemns them. It is a proclamation of Jesus' death on the cross, and a promise of forgiveness to all who have faith in him. Various churches have different practices and different understandings of the Lord's Supper, but on this we all agree: The bread and the cup represent what Jesus has done for us. And every time we take Communion, we do it in remembrance of him.

WE'RE IN THIS TOGETHER
(1 Cor. 11:17-28)

I'm guessing that many of the readers of Paul's first letter to the Corinthians at first did not appreciate what Paul had to say. Sensing a culture of indifference in the Corinth church, he wrote this letter to address his concerns. The underlying issue was divisions in the church. Factions had developed, perhaps along social class lines. This was particularly evident in their observance of the Lord's Supper, which followed a common meal. Because there were no church buildings back then, Christians would gather in private homes for worship, instruction, and fellowship. Those gatherings, which probably took place in the homes of more affluent members, could include 30–40 people.

The meetings would often involve eating together, and then sharing the Lord's Supper—a first-century potluck, if you will. People would bring food and then share it community style. But what had begun as a beautiful expression of Christian fellowship had degenerated into an ugly example of rude and insensitive behavior. Some of the better-off members of the church were arriving early and eating all the food, leaving less affluent later-arrivers to go hungry. Further, some members were missing the whole point of their gathering, drinking so much wine that they became drunk.

Paul wrote to confront those abuses, and to remind the Corinthian church what Christian fellowship is all about. He told the early arrivers that if eating and drinking were what they were most concerned with, then they should eat and drink at home. Then Paul reminded them what the Lord's Supper is all about: The bread and the cup are symbols of Christ's body and blood, sacrificed for the forgiveness of our sins. The selfless sacrifice of Jesus on the cross was in stark contrast to the selfish and self-indulgent attitude of some people in the Corinthian church. That's why Paul told them to examine themselves so that they would not eat or drink in an unworthy manner.

Sometimes we call the Lord's Supper "Communion," because it is a sign of our communion with God and our communion with one another. The Greek word that captures the meaning of our communion is *koinonia*, meaning fellowship, or partnership, or sharing. The church should be characterized by koinonia, by fellowship and partnership and sharing. The quality of our life together should be characterized by respect, concern, and compassion for each other. Because God loves us, we love each other. And we love each other by the way we treat each other. We do to others as we would have them do to us. We love our neighbors as we love ourselves. Sharing the Lord's Supper is a sign of our communion with one another.

Lauren Carstensen is the founding director of the Stanford Center on Longevity. In a column she wrote in the February 12, 2015 issue of *Time* magazine, Lauren stated that "baby boomers are isolating themselves as they age." I'm a baby boomer, as are an estimated 75 million of my fellow Americans. We baby boomers are an army of gray-haired people. Some of us are grayer than others, and some of us have more hair than others. We are better educated than any previous generation. Most of us have an emotional intelligence that has improved as we have aged, and most of us have a wisdom that has grown with age. We tend to be slower to anger, more prone to see silver linings, and more likely to forgive and forget. (This is not just my opinion; it is backed by a large body of research.)

Yet, in spite of all that the baby boomer generation has to offer, we are far less socially engaged than our predecessors were at our age 20 years ago. Boomers are less likely to participate in community groups or to be involved with religious organizations than were our counterparts a generation ago. Boomers are less likely to be married and less likely to talk with their neighbors frequently, and also report weaker ties with family and friends.

Researchers are trying to explain these patterns of social disengagement. Perhaps it is a byproduct of rejecting family values and traditions. Not coincidentally, boomers are the most-divorced generation in American history. Whatever the reasons, baby boomers are less socially engaged. And that is to our detriment. Many studies have shown a link between social engagement and health and longevity. Social isolation is a risk factor for early mortality. Health suffers as people withdraw from meaningful human interaction. On the other hand, people who are engaged in meaningful relationships are typically healthier, happier, and more productive.

Almost all of us know people who don't go to church or who have dropped out of church. Maybe they think they can relate to God without organized religion. Maybe they think they can maintain some kind of spirituality on their own. But they are missing a key benefit to church involvement: meaningful relationships with other people. Facebook is no substitute for face-to-face relationships. In fact, some studies have found the more time people spend on social networking sites, the more depressive symptoms they exhibit. Church involvement helps us to be socially engaged.

Another benefit to church involvement is the opportunity it gives us to participate in meaningful activities, such as helping other people. Studies have found that people are happier when they take part in meaningful service activities rather than when they focus only on themselves. Studies have found that people derive more long-term satisfaction from generosity than from self-indulgence. Doing good for someone else can help us to feel better about ourselves. So, in demonstrable ways, church involvement is not only good for the soul, but also good for our emotional well-being.

In his book *Deeply Woven Roots*, Gary Gunderson takes note of the root system of redwood trees. He says the trees become "giant" because their roots are woven together. They grow to be so tall because their roots become a network, supporting each other. Each tree relies on the other trees around it for stability. In like manner, we in the church are woven together through the root system of our common faith. As we share our life together, we support one another in good times and in bad, in sunshine and in rain, in calm and stormy gales. No one has to stand alone, for we stand together in the forest of God's love. We are deeply rooted in our faith, and our roots are interwoven through the fellowship of the church. Every time that we share the Lord's Supper, we remember what Jesus did for us, and we express our communion with each other in the fellowship of the church.

A LIFE WORTHY
(1 Cor. 11:23-28)

My grandmother had high expectations for her three grandchildren—my sister, my brother, and me. She expected us to go to church, to do well in school, to have good manners, to be kind and courteous, and to respect our elders. Much of who we became was due to the expectations our grandmother had for us. She was a soft-spoken, Christian lady, but the force of her personality made us want to please her. We would have done almost anything to live in a manner worthy of her love.

Perhaps you have had someone in your life who cared so much about you that they challenged you to be the best you could be. Paul had that attitude toward the early Christian churches. He was almost like a grandparent to them. He loved them and was proud of them, but he also had high expectations for them. He challenged them to be the best Christians they could be. In several of his letters—including to the Christians at Ephesus, Philippi, Colossae, and Thessalonica—Paul challenged them to live in accordance with their calling.

- Lead a life worthy of the calling to which you have been called (Eph. 4:1).
- Live your life in a manner worthy of the gospel of Christ (Phil. 1:27).
- Lead lives worthy of the Lord (Col. 1:10).
- Lead a life worthy of God (1 Thess. 2:12).

Paul was concerned that the people to whom he wrote lived a life worthy of their calling as Christians.

In his first letter to the church at Corinth, Paul expressed concern that the Christians there were living in an unworthy manner. Corinth was a Greek city, strategically situated on the isthmus connecting the Peloponnesus peninsula with mainland Greece. Because Corinth overlooked ports on both the Adriatic and Aegean seas, it was a wealthy center of commerce and a cosmopolitan city, drawing its population from Greeks, Romans, and many other nationalities. Corinth also had a Jewish community, and Paul had begun the Christian work there by preaching in the synagogue. Soon, however, Jewish opposition to his message forced the Christians to meet in private homes.

Although the church contained some Jewish converts, most of the members of the church in Corinth were from Gentile backgrounds. As it turned out, Paul had more problems with the church at Corinth than with perhaps any other Christian group. The main problem was a lack of unity in the church. There were serious divisions.

The church was divided over loyalty to various preachers—including Paul, Peter, and Apollos—while some people said they were only loyal to Christ. There were divisions over speaking in tongues and other charismatic gifts. There were divisions between the rich and the poor, and over the role of women in the church. There were divisions over the influence of philosophical teachings, such as Greek Gnosticism. Corinth was Paul's reality check. Whenever he was tempted to idealize the church, all he had to do was go back to Corinth.

The disunity in the Corinthian church was shamefully apparent in the way its members observed the Lord's Supper. Instead of worshipping in a church building, they would gather in homes to share a meal and then observe the Lord's Supper. But abuses had crept into what was supposed to be a "love feast." Some members of the church drank so much wine during dinner, they were intoxicated by the time they had the Lord's Supper. Some wealthy members would arrive early and eat all the food, while the poorer members who had to work later would arrive and have nothing left to eat. To put a stop to these abuses, Paul wrote to correct whoever "eats the bread or drinks the cup of the Lord in an unworthy manner. Examine yourselves, and only then eat of the bread and drink of the cup" (1 Cor. 11:27-28).

The Lord's Supper serves as our reality check—it helps us take stock, to see if we are living up to our Christian profession. Please notice: Paul does not say we are to examine ourselves to see if we are worthy to receive the Lord's Supper. None of us is worthy of that. We examine ourselves not to see if we are qualified to receive the Lord's Supper, but to see if we are living in a manner worthy of the gospel. And if not, we use the Lord's Supper as an occasion to recommit our lives to Christ. We examine ourselves to see where we need to repent, where we need God's forgiveness and help to live more worthy lives. This is the paradox of the Lord's Supper: the only way we can qualify ourselves to take Communion is to admit that we are unworthy to do so. Once we do that, we are in a position to accept God's forgiveness and grace.

Babette's Feast is the story of a French chef who left Paris to live and work in the home of two sisters in Norway. Their home is a joyless place because the two sisters were raised by a strict father who was the town minister. The father has long since died, but the sisters continue to be influenced by his rigid puritanical expectations for them. As the cook for these two straightlaced sisters, Babette works incognito, preparing plain and simple meals according to their instructions. No one knows that Babette worked in one of the finest restaurants in Paris or that Babette has the knowledge and the culinary skill to prepare a banquet fit for a king.

Babette lives with the hope of one day returning to France. Every year she buys a ticket in the French lottery, hoping to win enough money to buy her way home. Incredibly, after years of humble service, Babette does win the lottery and its prize of 10,000 francs. But instead of immediately booking passage back to France, Babette offers to prepare a meal to commemorate the birthday anniversary of the sisters' father, the pastor-founder of their small Norwegian community. The two sisters are not enthusiastic about a fancy dinner, but they cannot figure out how to gracefully decline without hurting Babette's feelings, so they accept. Babette happily plunges into her preparations for the feast. She orders special ingredients and the best wine. She hires young men to serve as waiters and wine stewards. Then the evening arrives for the meal.

Serendipitously, a guest is visiting the community, a famous general who just happens to be staying with his aunt, a neighbor and friend to the sisters. Of course, the general and his aunt are invited to share in the dinner. All through the meal, it is the general who recognizes the quality of what they are eating and drinking. The general is astonished by the fine wines, turtle soup, and extraordinary quail he had only tasted one time before—in an exclusive restaurant in Paris. Repeatedly, the general expresses astonishment that such food should be served in such a modest home. Gradually, even the sisters begin to join in the enjoyment of the meal. Indeed, as they share such a glorious bounty, they find themselves drawn together and connected in a way they would not have dreamed of before. After the evening is over, the sisters learn that Babette will not be returning to Paris after all. She has spent the entire 10,000 francs on the extravagant feast.

When we share the Lord's Supper, we come to God's table to share an extravagant feast. The bread and the cup represent the one who came as a servant to live among us and who gave his all for us. As we eat the bread and drink the cup, may we live worthy of his extravagant love.

QUESTIONS FOR DISCUSSION/REFLECTION

1. In what way is the Lord's Supper in three tenses: past, present, and future?
2. What is the "new covenant" that the Lord's Supper represents?
3. What is the purpose of examining ourselves before we partake of the Lord's Supper?
4. What does it mean "to proclaim the Lord's death until he comes"?
5. What does it mean to "do this in remembrance of me"?

CHAPTER 6

THE LOVE CHAPTER
(1 Cor. 13:4-13)

Love is patient, love is kind. It does not envy, it does not boast, it is not proud. It does not dishonor others, is not self-seeking, is not easily angered, keeps no record of wrongs. Love does not delight in evil but rejoices with the truth. It always protects, always trusts, always hopes, always perseveres. Love never fails. And now these three remain: faith, hope and love. But the greatest of these is love.

(1 Cor. 13:4-8a, 13 NIV)

First Corinthians 13 is often called "The Love Chapter." It is all about love—but not romantic love, or familial love, or friendship love. It is all about God's love, and the ways God wants us to love each other. Chapter 13 comes after Paul's discussion of spiritual gifts in chapter 12. In a sense, it is a conclusion to the discussion of spiritual gifts. The greatest gift of the Spirit is not prophecy or speaking in tongues, but love. This message was especially powerful and appropriate, given the divisive issues in the Corinthians church. Paul wrote often about faith, hope, and love (Rom. 5:1-5; Gal. 5:5-6; Col. 1:4-5; 1 Thess. 1:3, 5:8). But as he said in 1 Corinthians 13:13, "the greatest of these is love."

Paul was talking about *agape* love. Although it is a rather obscure word in secular Greek, in the Bible, *agape* is the most-used word for love. It occurs in the New Testament some 250 times. According to Paul, *agape* is the highest and purest form of love. This type of love should be the foundation for every relationship.

THE GREATEST IS LOVE
(1 Cor. 13:4-7, 13)

My wife Linda likes to remind me about our first Valentine's Day date before we were married. I took her to a nursing home. We also went out to dinner, but it is the nursing home part of the date that she likes to talk about. (Don't accuse me of being unromantic. At least it was memorable. How many Valentine dates do you remember?) We went to the nursing home so I could take some photos of a Valentine's Day party for the residents. I had promised to help a seminary classmate who was doing a pastoral care internship at the nursing home. Linda was getting an early introduction into what being a pastor's wife would be like.

I'm not sure who came up with the idea of Valentine's Day, but it has become a boon to florists and jewelers and stores that sell candy and greeting cards. Probably more married couples celebrate their wedding anniversary on Valentine's Day than any other day of the year. There are several myths about the origin of Valentine's Day (and its namesake, St. Valentine), although no one knows exactly how it came about. But who could argue with having a day devoted to love?

The problem is not with a day devoted to love, but rather that we have a muddled and overly romanticized notion of love in our culture. Too often we have confused romance with love. We have defined love as a feeling of the heart, rather than what love really is—namely, a commitment of the will. The love that is depicted in fairy tales somehow fails to correspond with our real-life experiences in real-life relationships.

Paul used the Greek word *agape* for love. Interestingly, this word was used sparingly by writers in secular Greek literature. More commonly used were *eros* (romantic love) and *philia* (family love). Paul and other New Testament writers widely used *agape* for God's love, and for the love that Christians are to have for one another. Jesus made *agape* the centerpiece of his teachings. "Love one another as I have loved you," he said. "Love your enemies." "Love your neighbor as yourself." Jesus was not talking about feelings. He was talking about attitudes and actions. Love is something we do, not just something we feel.

The church in Corinth was lacking in love. Scholars believe that Paul wrote at least four letters to the Corinthians, perhaps more than he wrote to any other church, probably because the Corinthian Christians needed a lot of help. People in the church didn't get along. They were fussing and fighting. The church was riven with jealousy and strife. Paul was deeply concerned about the lack of love among the members of the church in Corinth. One product of Paul's deep concern is the 13th chapter of his first letter to the Corinthians, sometimes called "The Love Chapter." Often read at weddings, surely this kind of love is appropriate for marriage, but it is much broader than the relationship between husbands and wives. This is the kind of love that Christians are to have in all relationships. Very briefly, let's review what Paul said about love.

"Love is patient; love is kind" (v. 4a).

While I was writing this piece, I received a call from a telemarketer. Unfortunately, I was neither patient nor kind with the caller who interrupted me. He called at a most inopportune time when I was in the midst of receiving some fresh insights, and his call broke my train of thought. I tried to be polite, but when I found out he was selling something, I brought our conservation to a halt as quickly as possible so I could get back to my writing.

Now, I'm sure telemarketers are used to having abrupt endings to their sales calls. But the experience reminded me that I am not always patient and kind. However, love is patient and kind. The love of God is patient and kind, and God wants us to be patient and kind with one another.

"Love is not envious or boastful or arrogant or rude. It does not insist on its own way; it is not irritable or resentful; it does not rejoice in wrongdoing, but rejoices in the truth" (vv. 4b-6).

Ben Crenshaw is a famous professional golfer. He twice won the Masters, one of the four men's professional major golf championships. He was captain of the Ryder Cup, a team competition between professional golfers from America and those from Europe. He is widely regarded as having one of the best putting strokes of all time. On the golf course, he was a fierce competitor. But his nickname is "Gentle Ben," because at heart he is a gentle person; he treats other people with kindness and respect.

As his playing career was ending, Ben Crenshaw began to gain renown as a golf course architect. He and his partner have designed some of the finest contemporary golf courses. His philosophy of golf course architecture reflects his philosophy of life. When asked to comment on his course-design work, he said: "Your work over a lifetime tells a story. We try to make a course look like it has been there a long time. It's very simple to us: Does this raw ground look like you can introduce golf on it in a peaceful way?"[1] I don't know anything about Ben Crenshaw's religious convictions, but his desire to fashion the land into a golf course without violence reveals his character. Such is the nature of love. It is thoughtful, gentle, and considerate of others.

"Love bears all things, believes all things, hopes all things, endures all things" (v. 7).

Love is gentle, but love is also strong. Love never gives up. Love outlives hurt, disappointment, sorrow, and every other negative experience of life. Notice that Paul says all this about love, not about us. In and of ourselves, we are not always kind and patient and forgiving and self-giving and enduring. But God's love encompasses all these characteristics. And when we receive God's love into our hearts, an amazing thing begins to take place: we become more like Jesus, whose very nature was love.

Paul is not saying here to become a more loving person. We don't have the power within ourselves to do this. Rather, Paul is saying to allow God's love to grow within yourself. The more we give ourselves to God, the more we allow God's love to become the dominant theme of our lives. So, it's not just a matter of making up our minds to be more patient, kind, forgiving. It's a matter of giving ourselves more fully to God and allowing God's love to make us more like Christ.

According to the traditions of the Roman Catholic Church, there were at least three saints named Valentine, all of whom were martyred for their faith. Perhaps the original St. Valentine was a priest who served the church in Rome during the third century AD under the Emperor Claudius II. The emperor decided that single men would make better soldiers for his army, so he decreed that young men would not be allowed to marry. St. Valentine refused to obey such an unjust law. As a priest, he continued to perform marriage ceremonies in secret. When the emperor found out about his defiance, Valentine was arrested, tortured, and eventually executed. The traditional date for his death was February 14, 270. The story of St. Valentine is a far cry from red roses and candy hearts, but it gets at the real meaning of love. Love is not just something you feel; love is something you do. "For God so loved the world that he gave his own Son" (John 3:16). Because of Jesus, faith and hope abide, but the greatest is love.

THE GREATEST GIFT
(1 Cor. 13:4-7, 13)

My wife Linda and I seldom go "all out" when it comes to celebrating our wedding anniversary. But one year, we outdid ourselves. We began the day by exchanging greeting cards. Linda's card to me featured Snoopy and Woodstock. My card to her came from the dollar store. Then we went on with our usual Saturday chores. Linda went shopping at two grocery stores, and I stayed at home and did the dishes and the laundry. But the big event was a nice dinner that evening at Jerry's Seafood.

Jerry's is pricey. In true Salmon fashion, we ordered the cheapest entrees on the menu. Linda had the baby crab bomb, and I had the halibut (just for the halibut). There were no appetizers, no extra sides, no dessert, and we had water to drink. Still, the bill came to more than $68. Fortunately, I had a $50 Jerry's gift certificate I had won in a charity golf tournament, so it wasn't quite such a hit to the credit card. After dinner we came home and watched TV, and I went over my sermon for Sunday. That was our exciting 39th wedding anniversary. Don't accuse us of being unromantic!

The truth is, any day I spend with Linda is a celebration. We have been married 44 years, and they have been the best years of my life. Linda and I first met when I was a student at the Baptist seminary in Louisville, Kentucky. Because I had to miss a semester due to illness, I didn't graduate when the rest of my class did. So, while most of my classmates were preparing to begin their ministerial careers, I had another semester to go. As a distraction, I accepted an invitation from a friend to take part in a dramatic production at a church on the east side of the city. I had never been to that church before. In fact, had it not been for the drama, I probably never would have gone to that church. As it turned out, a pretty, young woman named Linda was the star of the drama. I had a bit part. On the last night, after the performance and the cast party, I finally worked up the courage to ask her out. It was gutsy on my part, because Linda was older than I and she was a young widow with a three-year-old daughter. But I hoped she would give me a chance. She did, and she has continued giving me a chance for 44 years.

What does it take for a marriage to last this long? Or in the case of our friends Esther and Stanley Jacknewitz, what does it take for a marriage to last more than 60 years? To put it simply, it takes a lot of love. Now, the kind of love I'm talking about is not just romantic love, although it often begins that way. The kind of love I'm talking about is more than that. It's the kind of love Paul wrote about in our scripture passage.

"Love is patient; love is kind; love is not envious or boastful or arrogant or rude. It does not insist on its own way, it is not irritable or resentful, it does not rejoice in wrongdoing, but rejoices in the truth. It bears all things, believes all things, hopes all things, endures all things" (1 Cor. 13:4-7).

When Paul wrote these words about love, he wasn't just talking about marriage, although it certainly applies to marriage. His main concern was the quality of life in the community in the church in Corinth. Paul had received troubling reports of divisions in the church. Some of the divisions were theological in nature, some were based on social standing, and some were grounded in petty and self-centered behavior. Paul was upset about the lack of unity in the church at Corinth. Some people in the church were acting selfishly, without regard for the feelings and needs of their fellow church members.

So, Paul wrote his first letter to the Corinthians to address some of the causes of division, and to remind them what true Christian community is all about. In 1 Corinthians 13, Paul wrote about love. The word he used for love is not *eros* (Greek for romantic love) nor *philos* (Greek for family love), but *agape* (Greek for God's love). Paul used the word *agape* nine times in this chapter alone, focusing on the love that believers are to have for one another. Earlier in chapter 12, Paul mentioned various gifts of the Spirit. These include wisdom, knowledge, faith, healing, working miracles, prophecy, discernment, speaking in tongues, and the interpretation of tongues. In Corinth the exercise of these spiritual gifts was leading to divisions rather than unity. Some people, because they had certain gifts, thought they were better Christians than others in the church.

Paul compared the members of the church to the parts of the human body. Just as the body has many different parts, so the church has many different members. Just as every part of the human body is important, every member of the church is important. Paul wrote: "If one member suffers, all suffer together with it; if one member is honored, all rejoice together with it. Now you are the body of Christ, and individually members of it" (1 Cor. 12:26-27). God has appointed many roles in the church, and God has given many gifts to the members of the church. Paul concluded by saying that God's greatest gift to us is the gift of love.

Paul's point is that love is not just something we feel. Love is something we do. Love is expressed by the way we act toward one another. Paul gave some specific examples of what love looks like in action. For instance, love is patient and kind. Even when we don't feel like being patient and kind, if we exercise the gift of love, we move from being self-centered to being other-centered; we place the needs of the other person above our own needs. This is key for a marriage, and key for all close relationships. Of course, it only works if both people do it. If one person is patient and kind and the other person is pushy and mean, then the relationship can become manipulative and abusive. But as Christians we are called to love, to be patient and kind. In marriage, in family life, in church life, in all the significant relationships of our lives—we are to treat each other in a patient and kind way.

Most marriages would be better if the partners were simply more patient with each other and if they treated each other in a kind way. The same is true in the church. When we are patient and kind with each other, the quality of our life together is better. The same is true if we are not envious or boastful or arrogant or rude, or don't insist on our own way, or are not irritable or resentful. Respect and regard for others can go a long way toward peaceful, harmonious, and mutually satisfying relationships.

Two days after our 39th anniversary Linda and I kept the celebration going when we went to see the movie, *Free State of Jones*. It was a good choice for the 4th of July, because the movie is about freedom. Based on a true story—of which I had never heard—the movie is set in Mississippi during the Civil War, and continues into the years after the war when the South was trying to rebuild. The main characters are a Confederate Army deserter and a runaway slave. The movie is also a surprising love story.

The movie recounts how that in Mississippi during the Civil War some poor farmers and runaway slaves join in an uprising against the Confederacy. The Confederate Army deserter, Newton Knight, and the runaway slave, Rachel, not only find a common cause, but they also find each other. After the war they marry, and Rachel becomes one of a few black women in Mississippi to be a landowner.

The movie is well worth seeing. However, it is not easy to watch. There is much cruelty and brutality in the movie, especially on the part of the Confederates during the war, and on the part of the Ku Klux Klan after the war. In a way, the movie helps explain the racial disparities in our society and in our criminal justice system that exist even today.

But the movie is not all negative. There are acts of compassion and respect for human dignity, especially between runaway slaves such as Rachel and some of the white Southerners like Newt Knight. Underlying the compassion and respect for human dignity is an understanding of the true message of the Christian faith.

The essence of the Christian faith is love—God's love for us, as expressed in Jesus Christ, and our love for each other, as Christ calls us to do. Love is the greatest gift God has given to us, and love is the greatest gift we can give to each other. In marriage, in the family, in the church, in our larger society—it all boils down to love. Faith and hope are essential, but the greatest gift is love.

IT'S ALL ABOUT LOVE
(1 Cor. 13:4-8, 13)

Love is the basis of marriage. A marriage may endure without love, but it probably will not be a very happy one. With love, and in love, a marriage can not only endure, but also becomes the foundation for a lifetime of happiness. The Bible speaks of love not just as a feeling of the heart, but as a commitment of the will and as a steadfast devotion to the well-being of another person. Love involves far more than tender emotions. It involves patient attitudes and kind actions. Above all, love is something we do.

I've been conducting wedding ceremonies my entire adult life. I performed my first marriage ceremony when I was a student in college and a part-time youth minister at a church in Waco, Texas. A call came into the church office to see if a minister could come to a house outside of town and conduct a small wedding. Neither the pastor nor associate pastor wanted to do it, so they asked me.

At the time, any licensed minister could perform a wedding ceremony in Texas. I called my home church in Fort Worth and asked if it would be possible for them to license me to preach. They voted on it after a Wednesday night dinner, and then dropped my license in the mail. So, at age 20 I became qualified to perform weddings—at least in the state of Texas.

What did I know about performing a wedding ceremony? Not much. The pastor of my college church gave me a sample wedding ceremony he had used. I took it from there. I drove out into the country and found the farmhouse where the wedding was to take place. The ceremony lasted about 10 minutes, but it was legal, and the couple seemed satisfied. I think I read a passage from 1 Corinthians 13 during the ceremony. I've been using it in weddings ever since.

It used to be that when I would meet with a couple for the first time to discuss their upcoming wedding, I would ask them: Why are you getting married? It seemed like a logical question to ask. But then I discovered that I got the same answer every time: "We love each other." I don't ask that question anymore. We still discuss the meaning of marriage when I meet with a couple for premarital counseling, but I try to move the discussion beyond "we love each other."

Sometimes "we love each other" gives a couple a false sense of security. They imagine that because they love each other, their marriage is guaranteed to be good and to last. Statistics say otherwise. Just about every marriage in our culture begins in love, but many marriages do not continue in love. The problem is not love. The problem is that many couples don't know what real love is.

In his letter to the Corinthians, Paul gave a series of definitions of love. The definitions go way beyond romance: "Love is patient, love is kind. It does not envy, it does not boast, it is not proud. It does not dishonor others, it is not self-seeking, it is not easily angered, it keeps no record of wrongs."

It might surprise you to know that Paul wasn't thinking about marriage when he wrote those words in 1 Corinthians 13. While they certainly are appropriate for marriage and family life, Paul had more in mind: he was writing about life in the church.

The church in Corinth was a mess. It was marked by an absence of love. There was rivalry and jealousy in the congregation. The church was divided into factions, with groups pitted against each other. They argued about whether it was proper to eat food sacrificed to idols. Some of them brought lawsuits against their fellow church members. Some were tolerating sexual immorality. There was discourtesy and insensitivity. When they would gather for a common meal, the rich people would get there first and eat all the food, leaving nothing for the poorer members who arrived later. Some of them were making a mockery of the Lord's Supper by getting drunk on the wine. Some of them had the gift of tongues, the ecstatic prayer language that others could not understand. The tongues-speakers were lording it over the other church members who did not have that gift, as if they were somehow holier than the others. It was an ugly scene. Yet, it was to this discordant, dysfunctional collection of people that Paul addressed beautiful words about love.

Paul was not a starry-eyed sentimentalist. He knew that genuine love is hard. It requires patience, kindness, and forgiveness. It requires biting your tongue instead of lashing out in anger. It requires courtesy and consideration instead of rudeness and irritation. It requires unselfishness, instead of self-centeredness. In other words, love requires the spirit of Christ in all that we say and do.

No church has perfected the business of love. It is a constant challenge to respect each other and to treat each other with patience, kindness, courtesy, and consideration. It's a challenge not to speak in anger, nor keep a record of wrongs. It's a challenge to be unselfish, and to put the feelings and needs of others ahead of our own feelings and needs. But that is what love is about. Love is about treating others the way we would want to be treated.

Near the end of the love chapter Paul wrote, "When I was a child, I spoke like a child, I thought like a child, I reasoned like a child; when I became an adult, I put an end to childish ways." This was Paul's way of saying that love is a sign of spiritual maturity. The childish person is characterized by selfishness. The mature woman or man in Christ lives in love.

My friend Ron Brown, who used to serve on the staff of the Baptist Convention of Maryland/Delaware, became a consultant for churches in conflict. He would go into churches that were divided by conflict and seek to help them achieve some kind of resolution and reconciliation. Ron told me that there was no shortage of churches that needed his help. In fact, he trained 10 teams to go into troubled churches and try to help them resolve their differences. All 10 teams would be working with 10 different churches at any given time. I was grateful to learn that there are people like Ron and his teams who have the training, experience, and temperament to be conflict-resolution specialists. But if churches would take "the love chapter" seriously in the first place, Ron would happily have been out of a job.

Among medical researchers there is the perpetual quest for a "magic bullet"—a drug or treatment that can cure a disease. We seek a magic bullet for cancer, for heart disease, for every illness that brings suffering and death. But the magic bullet for human relationships has already been given: love. When we love each other the way that God loves us, our relationships will be happy and enduring. Why? Because love never ends. Love endures all things. Love doesn't give out. Love doesn't give up. Love doesn't stop. Whatever happens, love keeps on going. Why does love last?

First, love lasts because it is a choice. Love is not a momentary emotion, not a fleeting feeling, not a passing passion. Love is a choice, a conscious decision, a willing commitment. It is a basic attitude toward other people. Love lasts because it becomes a way of life.

Second, love lasts because it is from God. God's very nature is love. All that God is, all that God does, is love. When we live unselfishly, when we act self-sacrificially, somehow the power of God flows through us. When we make love the guiding principle of our lives, somehow, we participate in the very nature of God.

In his short story, "The Great Stone Face," Nathaniel Hawthorne tells how a little boy becomes a man. Growing up, the boy lives in the valley beneath a mighty mountain. On the side of the mountain, a great stone face is carved in the rock overlooking the valley. Every day the boy stares up at the great stone face. He admires it and is inspired by it. When the boy reaches adulthood, he discovers that the features of the great stone face have become his own. He has become that which he looked up to and admired. He has become his ideal.

We, too, become that which we look up to and admire. We become our ideal. And for us, the ideal that inspires us is not a nameless stone face on the side of a mountain, but a figure on a scaffold on a God-forsaken hill. If you want a perfect picture of love, that is it: Jesus on the cross. And the more we admire and follow that love, the more we will look like that.

QUESTIONS FOR DISCUSSION/REFLECTION

1. How is God's love different from human love?
2. Why does love never fail?
3. Why is love greater than faith and hope?
4. Is it possible to love all the time?
5. How does the love of God come to you?

NOTE

"Ben Crenshaw Sounds Off," *Golf Magazine*, February 2004, 116.

CHAPTER 7

WE DO NOT LOSE HEART
(2 Cor. 4:16-18)

So we do not lose heart. Even though our outer nature is wasting away, our inner nature is being renewed day by day. For this slight momentary affliction is preparing us for an eternal weight of glory beyond all measure, because we look not at what can be seen but at what cannot be seen.

(2 Cor. 4:16-18a NRSV)

In his "second" letter to the Corinthians, Paul begins by talking about some "affliction" he and his traveling companions have experienced in Asia. He references the "affliction" repeatedly in the opening verses of 2 Corinthians 1 (vv. 4, 6, 8) and then picks up the theme again in chapter 4: "We are afflicted in every way, but not crushed; perplexed, but not driven to despair; persecuted, but not forsaken; struck down, but not destroyed" (vv. 8-9). Paul later details some of the afflictions in 2 Corinthians 6:4-5 ("hardships, calamities, beatings, imprisonments, riots, labors, sleepless nights, hunger") and again in 2 Corinthians 11:23-27 (including imprisonments, floggings, lashings, beatings, stoning, shipwrecks, danger from many sources, sleeplessness, hunger, thirst, and exposure to the elements).

For Paul, all these afflictions were a sign that "we have this treasure in clay jars" or earthen vessels, meaning weaknesses and troubles and limitations are inherent in human life. Yet, we do not lose heart. "We have this treasure in clay jars, so that it may be made clear that this extraordinary power belongs to God and does not come from us" (2 Cor. 4:7). Paul deems all his hardships and sufferings to be a "slight momentary affliction" because it is "preparing us for an eternal weight of glory beyond all measure." In other words, this life is not all there is; this world is not all there is. What can be seen is only temporary. Our outer nature is wasting away, but our inner nature is being renewed day by day.

EARTHEN VESSELS
(2 Cor. 4:7-18)

He wasn't much to look at. If you saw him, you probably would have felt sorry for him. He was severely handicapped. He sat all day in a wheelchair. His body was thin and frail, his face without expression. The only movement he could make was to twitch his fingers. He could not do any of the things we take for granted. He could not feed himself. He could not dress himself. He could not even speak. He was paralyzed by a progressive, incurable disease, ALS, sometimes called Lou Gehrig's disease. To look at him you might have thought, "what a poor, pathetic, miserable wretch." But you would have been wrong.

This man I have described was Stephen Hawking, the world-famous theoretical physicist, cosmologist, and author of a number-one bestseller, *A Brief History of Time*. He held an endowed mathematics professorship at Cambridge University, a chair once held by Sir Isaac Newton, and was widely regarded as the most brilliant theoretical physicist since Albert Einstein. Yet, there he sat, a genius trapped in a broken-down, worn-out body—treasure in an earthen vessel.

From what we can tell, the apostle Paul wasn't much to look at either. The Bible doesn't say a lot about his appearance, but apparently Paul was not an imposing figure. In 2 Corinthians 10:10, Paul describes himself by quoting what other people say about him: "His letters are weighty and strong, but his bodily presence is weak, and his speech is contemptible." A description of Paul found in the second-century pseudepigraphal writing, *Acts of Paul* or *Apocryphal Acts*, is even more graphic: "short of stature, bald and bow-legged, with meeting eyebrows and a prominent nose" (not exactly a flattering portrait!).

On top of all that, Paul had other problems. Almost everywhere he went, Paul got knocked around. In 2 Corinthians 6, he lists some of the abuse he has endured: beatings, imprisonment, hunger, and more. In chapter 11, Paul writes that he received 39 lashes five times, was beaten with rods three times, was stoned, and three times was shipwrecked. (Talk about someone who was a glutton for punishment!) In addition, Paul had a thorn in the flesh. He had some physical ailment that tormented him. And yet, in spite of his appearance, the beatings and hardships, the thorn in the flesh, his weak body and "no account" speech, he too was treasure in an earthen vessel.

One summer when traveling home from the beach, Linda and I stopped at a factory outlet where a pottery store was offering a deal on some slightly blemished dishes. Because we could buy the pieces separately, we were able to purchase only the quantities we needed. We bought 14 dinner plates, 12 smaller plates, 16 bowls, and 4 cups. I figured we would not have to buy another plate or bowl or cup for the rest of our lives. I was wrong. I forgot that pottery pieces are earthen vessels. And earthen vessels are fragile—they get chipped, or cracked, or even broken.

Our lives are like that. We are fragile and susceptible to the wear and tear of years of use. Every time I go out to play tennis, I am reminded of that for the next two days. To be honest, most of us are blemished to begin with, and we don't necessarily get better with age. But Paul says not to worry. Though our outer natures are wasting away, our inner natures, our true selves, are being renewed day by day. There is something valuable in each of us that is not dependent on how we look or what status we have or what we can do. Unfortunately, we live in a society that tries to deny that.

Our society worships externals. The treasures of our culture are money, beauty, success, luxury, and power. I saw a bumper sticker that read, "the one who dies with the most toys wins." Jesus had a response to that: "Do not lay up for yourselves treasures on earth, which moths consume and rust destroys, but lay up treasures in heaven" (Matt. 6:19-20).

The folly of our age is that we have sought to give lasting value to things that do not last. We have mistaken the earthen vessels for the treasures they contain. I am not suggesting that we give away all our possessions or disregard our physical appearance or renounce achievement. But I am suggesting that we be careful not to make those things ultimate. Money cannot buy happiness; physical beauty will fade; power does not guarantee friendship or good health. As Paul wrote, "What can be seen is temporary, but what cannot be seen is eternal."

What does "treasure in earthen vessels" mean for us? For one thing, it affects how we look at other people. It means there is something of value in everyone, regardless of how they look, or what they do for a living, or where they come from, or how much they have, or any other external. Jesus recognized that. He could look beneath the externals of a woman or a man and see the real person. Jesus could value people for who they really were, and for who they could become.

The movie, *Suspect*, is a story about human worth. Set in Washington, D.C., a woman has been murdered, her throat slashed. A homeless man, a deaf Vietnam vet with PTSD, is the prime suspect. All the evidence seems to point in his direction: he was seen sleeping in the victim's car on the night of her murder, with the victim's purse in his possession, along with a large knife. In addition, he has a history of violent behavior and looks as if he could have done it—a hulking figure with ragged clothes, long stringy hair, a shaggy beard, and a penetrating stare.

Everyone figures it will be a quick trial, and a quick conviction. Yet, the defense attorney sees something in this homeless man that others cannot see. She sees a man with faults and flaws, and yet, a man who is innocent. So, she dares to investigate further the circumstances of the crime. She sees treasure in an earthen vessel, value in a man whom everyone else thinks is worthless. She dares to care. And her caring helps lead to proving the man's innocence.

If we take Paul's words seriously, we look at other people differently. We look beneath the externals and find value in the real person. Not only does this affect how we look at others, but it also affects how we look at ourselves. All too often, we see only half of the picture; we see only the earthen part of our natures—our failings, our shortcomings, our weaknesses—and we get down on ourselves. We need to recognize the other half of who we are. Yes, we are imperfect and flawed, but by the grace of God, we are not worthless. There is treasure in each of us—something of value, something precious, something special. It is the image of God, the power of God, in our lives.

Maybe you remember the American speed skater, Dan Jansen. During the 1988 Winter Olympics he was favored to win the gold medal in two events, but during both races he fell on the ice and failed to finish. What a disappointment—years of training, discipline, and sacrifice wiped out in a few seconds. And yet, Dan Jansen was not devastated. His 27-year-old sister had died on the morning of the first race, after a long battle against leukemia. Dan was thinking about her, and his family, and his faith, and that put his failure to win a medal into perspective.

By the way, Dan Jansen did not lose heart. Dan finally won his gold medal in the 1994 Winter Olympics. But perhaps his greatest accomplishment was establishing the Dan Jansen Foundation, in memory of his sister Jane, for the purpose of aiding individuals and families affected by cancer.

Yes, we are afflicted, but not crushed; we are struck down, but not destroyed. The things we see, the externals of life, will pass away. But the things we do not see, the eternal treasures, will last forever. No matter what happens, God is still God, and through the love of Christ we find the power to go on. For we have this treasure in earthen vessels, treasure that is only a foretaste of that eternal glory yet to come.

LIVING IN THE LIGHT OF ETERNITY
(2 Cor. 4:16-18)

US Airways Flight 696, originating in Ft. Myers, Florida, made an emergency landing at Dulles Airport near Washington, D.C. The plane was headed for Reagan National Airport, but a cockpit warning light indicated problems with the right landing gear. Because Dulles has longer runways and is better equipped to handle an emergency landing, the Boeing 737 was diverted there.

After the pilot alerted the 130 passengers that there was a problem, flight attendants began instructing passengers on how to open the emergency doors and how to brace themselves for a crash landing. Obviously, it was a terrifying time for everyone aboard. Some people were weeping; others were praying. An Arlington, Virginia man called his wife to tell her he loved her. A woman tried to get to her sister in another part of the plane to say goodbye. Flight attendants repeatedly yelled "Brace!" to the passengers crouched into emergency landing positions. A woman said, "it was eerie hearing babies crying and thinking this was the last sound you were going to hear."

The pilot did a touch-and-go maneuver to try to shake loose the stuck landing gear. With a half-dozen fire trucks and other emergency vehicles parking alongside the runway, the pilot landed on the left main gear and then lightly touched the right wheel on the runway just to test it. After that brief touchdown, the plane took off again and circled around for another landing. This time the plane came down on both sets of wheels and the landing gears held. It turned out that the problem had been with the warning indicator light, not the landing gear. But one passenger said later, "It's not often that you contemplate your own death."

Statistically, commercial airplane travel is one of the safest forms of transportation. In a normal year, millions of people fly safely. You are much more likely to be killed riding in an automobile than in an airplane. But that was little consolation to those 130 passengers on Flight 696 who thought they were going to die. When the flight attendants warned them that the right wing would likely scrape across the ground on impact, the passengers imagined the plane coming apart or disintegrating in a fireball or explosion. For many of them, their lives must have flashed before their eyes. They spent what they imagined could have been their final moments doing what they considered to be most important—praying, or saying goodbye to loved ones, or simply holding on to one another. No doubt, it was an experience they will never forget.

Most of us don't spend much time thinking about our own mortality. For most of us, the only time we think about death is at funerals, or maybe when we hear about some disaster. In our culture, thinking about death is considered morbid and unhealthy. But in reality, what is really unhealthy is to deny that which is inevitable.

Some years ago, when Linda and I were on vacation in Ireland, we took a drive one evening along an elevated stretch outside Clifden in Connemara called the Sky Road. On our way out of town the road ascended to a ridge along the cliff tops that looked out over the ocean. But coming back into town, we took the low road that came down near the shoreline. While the upper part of the Sky Road was narrow, with barely room for two vehicles to pass side by side, the lower part of the road was narrower still, with only one lane in some places.

As we were driving along the low road shortly before sunset, we saw a line of vehicles coming toward us. There was not room for traffic in both directions, so we pulled off into a driveway and watched as the vehicles passed by. The first vehicle appeared to be a hearse, with other cars following behind. It looked like a funeral procession. But that didn't make any sense. It was about 7:30 p.m. on a Sunday evening, and we were driving through a small community of farmhouses and cottages. Why would there be a funeral procession at that place and time? Then we realized they were bringing the body of the deceased to the family home for the wake. Probably the funeral mass would take place the next day in the village church. But the night before the funeral there would be a viewing in the home for family members and friends who wished to pay their final respects.

Years ago, such a practice was not uncommon in the United States, but now funeral homes are considered a more appropriate venue for dealing with death. Most of us probably would not want the body of a loved one in our homes overnight. Death is something we relegate to funeral homes and cemeteries, not something we bring home where we live. We would much rather think about life than about death. And we do a pretty good job pushing any thoughts about death to the deep recesses of our minds—until something happens and we have to think about it. But our Christian faith helps us to put death into a proper perspective. Our faith places death within the larger context of God's redemptive love, so that instead of living in the shadow of death, we can live in the light of eternity.[1]

Paul wrote about living in the light of eternity in 2 Corinthians 4. He made three basic affirmations. First, we are all in the process of dying: "our outer nature is wasting away." Whether slowly or quickly, we are all wasting away.

One morning I was going over some scheduling with our church secretary in her office when we heard a sudden loud bang. I stepped outside her office into the foyer to investigate. As I began to look around, I looked out through the glass doors to the front porch. There I saw a bird lying on its back on the doormat, twitching its legs and feathers, but otherwise not moving. I told our secretary that the bird must have flown into the glass door and knocked itself out. We watched for another moment, and the twitching stopped. The bird lay absolutely still. After a little while, I went out onto the porch and scooped up the dead bird with a snow shovel and carried its lifeless body into the woods behind the church.

That bird probably didn't wake up that morning and say to itself, "Today is the last day of my life." In fact, it must have been in vigorous health to be able to fly with such force into the glass door as to kill itself. In one moment, the bird was flying like the wind; in the next moment, it lay dying on the doormat. Through a fatal error in judgment, the bird crossed the line between life and death in an instant.

Life in this world is limited. We will not live forever on this earth. That applies to birds, and to humans too. For some, death approaches slowly over many months or years. For others, death is more sudden. But of this we are certain: we will all die. Even if we are in vigorous health right now, our outer nature is wasting away. That's the first affirmation Paul made.

But there is a second affirmation: this life is not all there is. Paul said, "even though our outer nature is wasting away, our inner nature is being renewed day by day."

God did not make us to live just for a short while upon this earth, but rather God made us for eternity. Our inner nature, our true selves, the persons we really are, was made to last forever. The Bible says that humans, apart from the rest of creation, were made in the image of God. Some interpreters say that relates to freedom and the ability to make meaningful choices. Others say it relates to the unique relationship that God wants to have with us. I would also suggest that being made in the image of God means that we were made for eternity.

God made us in such a way that the essence of who we are, our souls, our spirits, will not die when our bodies do. Our outer nature wastes away, but our inner nature is renewed day by day. For those who have placed their faith in Christ, we believe that Jesus has gone to prepare a place for us, so that after we die, we can be with him in heaven. That's why Paul wrote, "this slight momentary affliction is preparing us for an eternal weight of glory." This life is not all there is. We will all die, but death is not the end for those who die in Christ.

Third, because we are all in the process of dying, and because this life is not all there is, we are to focus on the eternal, not the temporary. The temporary things of life can be seen, but the eternal things cannot be seen. The problem for most of us is that we focus almost exclusively on what can be seen, rather than on what we cannot see. We can see our possessions, the places where we live and work, the things around us, and too often, that is our focus. But those things that cannot be seen—faith, hope, and love—are what really last.

If we live in the light of eternity, we focus on what cannot be seen. Our priorities change. Our values are different. We come to recognize that relationships are more important than possessions. We re-evaluate how we use our time and where we devote our energies. We come to understand that character is more important than reputation, that true wealth is treasures in heaven rather than treasures on earth. Rick Warren wrote: "Living in the light of eternity...will color how you handle every relationship, task, and circumstance. Suddenly many activities, goals, and even problems that seemed so important will appear trivial, petty, and unworthy of your attention. The closer you live to God, the smaller everything else appears."[2]

What would it mean for your life if you started living in the light of eternity? I hope it would mean that you would focus more on what is eternal, rather than just on what is temporary. I hope it would mean that you make the will of God the highest ambition of your life. I hope it would mean that you love God with all your heart and mind and strength, and that you love your neighbor as you love yourself. I hope it would mean that you begin and end every day with God, and in the moments in between the beginning and the end of every day, you try to follow Jesus.

Living in the light of eternity means that we do not fear the shadow of death. For we who believe in Christ know that our loving heavenly Father is waiting for us on the other side. The Father is waiting, with arms open wide, ready to welcome us to our eternal home.

LIVE LIKE YOU WERE DYING
(2 Cor. 4:16-18)

I am not a big fan of country music. Even though I grew up in Texas, my family was into classical music, jazz, and Broadway musicals, so that was what I listened to as a child. Later, I developed an interest in pop music and Motown and folk rock, but I never got into country. One day, however, while stuck in traffic I began station-surfing on the radio. I heard a country song sung by the popular artist Tim McGraw that got my attention. Since I generally don't listen to country music, the song was new to me, though it has long been a staple on country music charts. The song is titled, "Live Like You Were Dying." The lyrics go:

> He said "I was in my early 40s, with a lot of life before me
> When a moment came that stopped me on a dime
> I spent most of the next days, looking at the x-rays
> Talkin' 'bout the options and talkin' 'bout sweet times"
>
> I asked him when it sank in, that this might really be the real end
> How's it hit ya when you get that kind of news?
> Man whatcha do?
>
> He said:
>
> "I went skydiving
> I went rocky mountain climbing
> I went two point seven seconds on a bull named 'Fu Man Chu'
> And I loved deeper
> And I spoke sweeter
> And I gave forgiveness I'd been denyin'"
>
> And he said: "Some day I hope you get the chance
> To live like you were dyin'"

The song captured my imagination because it tells a story that could happen to any of us. What would you do if you went to the doctor and were diagnosed with a terminal illness?

I doubt that you would go sky diving, or even Rocky Mountain climbing, and I'm almost certain that you would not want to ride 2.7 seconds on a bull named Fu Man Chu. But if you were given a death sentence, my guess is that you would take a hard look at your life and make some intentional decisions about how you would live the rest of your days.

I learned that the song had special meaning for Tim McGraw, because as he was preparing to record it, his own father was dying of brain cancer. Tug McGraw was a baseball pitcher for the New York Mets and Philadelphia Phillies. It was Tug McGraw who helped the "Miracle Mets" to their World Series victory in 1969, and who threw the last pitch for the Phillies in their World Series win in 1980. But for most of his childhood, Tim McGraw was not a part of his father's life.

Tim McGraw didn't even know that Tug McGraw was his father until he was 11 years old. Tim was rummaging around in his mother's closet when he found his birth certificate. Tim had assumed that his mother's former husband, a part-time truck driver, was his father. What his mother had not told him was that Tim was conceived out of wedlock as a result of a summer romance that she had with a minor-league baseball player named Tug. She married the truck driver a year after Tim was born, so Tim had no idea who his real father was. After Tim discovered his birth certificate, his mother told him the story and made contact with Tug. His mother took Tim from their home in Louisiana to Houston when the Phillies were in town for a series with the Astros. There Tim met his biological father for the first time. It was a brief and awkward meeting, with Tug expressing doubts that Tim was really his son. Tim did not see his father again for a long time. Tim wrote letters to Tug during his teenage years, but Tug never answered.

Then, after Tim graduated from high school, he insisted on seeing Tug again, for what he thought would be their final meeting. They met in a hotel lobby in Houston. When Tug saw this strapping young man—a high school baseball, football, and basketball player—Tug knew instinctively that this was indeed his son. For the first time in his life, Tim began to have a relationship with his father. Tug offered to pay for some of Tim's expenses at Northeast Louisiana University, and Tim started college with the intent to play baseball and eventually become a lawyer. While in college, Tim bought a guitar at a pawn shop and taught himself to play by listening to records and watching Country Music Television. Eventually, he learned enough songs to make some money playing for tips at bars and clubs. Tim decided to drop out of college after two years and move to Nashville so he could follow his dream of making music for a living.

Tug thought it was a bad idea for Tim to drop out of school and chase after such an improbable career, but Tug had always been a free spirit himself, so he couldn't blame his son too much. Tug was not enthusiastic about Tim's fledgling music career, but he gave his son enough money to buy a U-Haul trailer and an old Dodge van, so Tim could take his show on the road. After a few years of rocky communication, Tim came to terms with his father's sometimes irresponsible personality and the two grew closer. Tim's career began to take off, and he married another rising country music star, Faith Hill. Eventually, Tim and Faith would have three daughters, and Tim vowed to be the kind of father he had never known. Tim said, "Being a good father is the most important job you'll ever have. That's part of my makeup now—to make sure I'm a lot better dad than I ever had."[3]

As time passed, Tim and Tug began to make up for lost time. Tim and Faith were there when Tug was inducted into the Phillies Hall of Fame in 1999, even presenting Tug with a Harley-Davidson motorcycle in honor of the occasion. Then, in 2003, Tug was diagnosed with brain cancer. He was treated at the Duke University Medical Center, but the cancer was too advanced to be cured. Tug McGraw passed away in January 2004 at Tim's home outside of Nashville. Tug's final days were spent with the son he had not even acknowledged for the first 18 years of Tim's life. Later that month, Tim recorded the song, "Live Like You Were Dying."

In 2 Corinthians 4:16-18, Paul wrote that as Christians we are to live like we are dying, for indeed we are. He said that what can be seen is only temporary, but what cannot be seen is eternal. But instead of being afraid of death or denying our mortality, Paul said we do not lose heart. Even though our outer nature is wasting away, our inner nature is being renewed day by day.

What would it mean for us to live like we were dying? What changes would we make, what actions would we take, if we knew we had only a limited time left upon this earth?

I suppose for every individual this is a very personal question, but it seems there are a couple of things we could say that would apply to all of us. First, if we were to truly live like we were dying, we would focus more on what cannot be seen than on what can be seen. In other words, we would focus more on the things of the spirit than on the material things of life, understanding that material things do not last. We would focus more on the things of the spirit because only the spiritual will last into eternity.

Bob Roberts, who served in mission efforts for the American Baptist Churches USA, wrote in a column advising preachers to preach against storage units. That's right— storage units! Bob said that most storage units contain items that started out in living quarters, were moved to the basement, then to the garage, and finally into rented storage units. Most people in our culture have more stuff than they know what to do with. Bob said that a new air-conditioned, climate-controlled storage unit was built near where he lived in Orlando, Florida. When he drove by the new air-conditioned storage units on a hot, humid day, he saw a group of homeless people sitting around on park benches and steps and the ground. The homeless looked hot and tired and thirsty. Bob thought to himself how God's heart must be grieved by our mixed-up values. The excess stuff that people don't really need is housed in air-conditioned storage units, while homeless people swelter in the noonday sun. If we lived like we were dying, we would focus more on the needs of people than on accumulating more and more things.

Another way that we might live like we were dying would be to focus more on personal relationships than on personal accomplishments. In the end, what will matter most to us are not the diplomas on the wall, the cars in the driveway, the commendations and promotions at work, the accolades and achievements, the size of our bank accounts and investment portfolios. In the end, what will matter most are the people we love, and the people who love us.

Tim McGraw became the honorary chairman of the Tug McGraw Foundation, dedicated to improving the quality of life for brain cancer patients. The Foundation made a $5 million gift to the Duke University Medical Center's Brain Tumor Center for research and treatment of brain cancer. Tim could not bring his father back, but he could do something to honor his father's memory. Every time Tim McGraw would sing "Live Like You Were Dying" in concert, near the end of the song he would tap his chest like his father used to do on the pitcher's mound, and point to the sky.

If we were to live like we were dying, we would focus more on personal relationships and less on personal achievements. We would focus more on the unseen things of the spirit and less on the material things of this earth. We would recognize that what really matters is not what we have achieved, but whom we have loved. If we were to live like we were dying, our priority would be on our relationships with other people and our relationship with God. The good news is that we don't have to wait to receive a dire diagnosis from the doctor to make some positive changes in our lives. We can begin right now to live for eternity.

And I loved deeper
And I spoke sweeter
And I gave forgiveness I'd been denyin'"

And he said: "Some day I hope you get the chance
To live like you were dyin'"

QUESTIONS FOR DISCUSSION/REFLECTION

1. In what ways is our "outer nature wasting away"?
2. In what ways is our "inner nature being renewed day by day"?
3. What is your "slight momentary affliction"?
4. What is the "eternal weight of glory" for you?
5. What is it that "cannot be seen" which is eternal?

NOTES

[1]"Living in the Light of Eternity" comes from the best-selling book by Rick Warren, *The Purpose Driven Life: What on Earth Am I Here For?* (Zondervan, 2002).

[2]Ibid., 37.

[3]Interview by Ben Fong-Torres, "Live for Today," *Parade*, August 22, 2004.

CHAPTER 8

ALL GOD'S CHILDREN
(Gal. 3:23-29)

> *You are all God's children through faith in Christ Jesus. All of you who were baptized into Christ have clothed yourselves with Christ. There is neither Jew nor Greek; there is neither slave nor free; nor is there male and female, for you are all one in Christ Jesus.*
> (Gal. 3:26-28 CEB)

We are one in Christ Jesus. We are not divided by race, or social status, or gender, or any other demarcation. Our baptism into Christ creates a radical unity. Human distinctions no longer separate us. This, of course, is the ideal.

In the Declaration of Independence, Thomas Jefferson wrote, "We hold these truths to be self-evident: that all men are created equal." Jefferson may have believed this noble principle, but he himself was a slaveowner, as were many of the founding fathers. If Jefferson had had his way, slavery would have been abolished when the United States became a sovereign nation. But the ideal of all men being created equal was just that—an ideal.

In reality, only white males, and probably only white males of means, were seen as equals. Women, Native Americans, African Americans, and other minorities were not given equal rights when America was founded, nor throughout most of American history. How could the founders justify such a contradiction? They used sexism and racism to explain the inferior status given to women and racial minorities. Sometimes they even appealed to certain verses in the Bible to try to substantiate this sexism and racism.

In his letter to the Galatians, Paul countered the racism and the sexism of his day, and ours. Racism and sexism were rampant in the ancient world. The Jews were notorious racists. Not only did they look down on other ethnic groups, but they also separated themselves from other races. The Jews were patriarchal in their attitude toward women. But along came a Jew named Jesus, and then came a Jew named Paul, and these two dared to challenge the bigotry of their Jewish culture. Jesus associated with people of other races and with women. His whole life was a rebellion against the racism and sexism of his culture. Taking his clue from Jesus, Paul targeted his ministry to non-Jews, whom the Jews derisively called "Gentiles." And Paul included a number of women among his co-workers. Jesus and Paul demonstrated by their lives that racism and sexism are wrong.

THE GREAT EQUALIZER
(Gal. 3:26-29)

In the short story "Harrison Bergeron" by Kurt Vonnegut, the year is 2081, and equality is the law of the land. The 210th, 211th, and 212th amendments to the Constitution have decreed that all people are to be equal in every way. And to carry out those laws, a government agency has been established to enforce that equality. This agency has gone to any length to make people equal. For example, those who are beautiful or handsome are required to wear ugly masks to make them no better than anyone else. Those who are strong or graceful are weighted down with chains and bags of buckshot so that they are on the same level as those who are weak or clumsy. People with good eyesight are made to wear thick glasses that distort their vision. And there is a special provision for those who are intelligent. The smart ones must wear an earpiece that emits a loud buzz every 10 seconds to interrupt any intelligent thoughts. Such is one man's vision of an equal society.

America was founded on the proposition that all persons are equal under the law and in the sight of God. Thomas Jefferson said so in the Declaration of Independence. It is ironic that at the time he wrote "all men are created equal," people were not treated equally at all. Slavery was a prominent part of the American landscape, and women were given second-class citizenship at best. Still, the United States of America was born with the ideal of equality, even though we have never quite lived up to it.

Equality is a noble ideal, a religious ideal, a biblical ideal. And yet, even in most churches, it is still only an ideal. The same was true in Paul's time. When Paul wrote in his letter to the Galatians that "there is no difference between Jews and Gentiles, between slaves and free men, between men and women," it was a revolutionary concept. Gentiles, slaves, and women were inferior to male Jews. The Jews were extremely prejudiced. Every morning the Jewish male prayed, "Thank God that I am not a Gentile or a slave or a woman." Even today, the words of Paul to the Galatians are revolutionary.

According to Paul, our relationship to Christ destroys those walls that separate blacks from whites, women from men, poor people from rich people. It's not a matter of developing a more tolerant attitude, nor of condescending to associate with other races or social classes. No, the walls that divide us are broken down because of our union with Christ.

The New Testament scholar Hans Dieter Betz wrote that the verses from Galatians were probably used in early Christian baptismal ceremonies. As new believers were being baptized, they were given the title "sons of God." This was a significant designation because the title "sons of God" was usually reserved for Jews at the Last Judgment. But in Galatians, Paul says that all persons—Jews and Greeks, slaves and free, men and women—all persons through baptism are "children of God." No one is superior because of their race or social class or gender. Every person can stand on equal footing because we are truly equal in Christ.

Most of us, in theory, believe that everyone is equal before God, but too often the old prejudices hang on. For many of us, the message has not made the complete journey from our heads to our hearts. Race relations and gender relations are still issues in our society.

In Kurt Vonnegut's short story, everyone is equal, but it is an equality based on bringing people down to the same level. In the Christian community, however, we are equal because Christ raises us up to the same level, the level of being called "children of God." Four words put all of us on the same plane. Four words give all of us a worth and a dignity beyond our deserving. Four words mean that no one is better than another, but that all of us are made better than we were. Four words: "Christ died for me."

An old country preacher had a saying: "The ground is level at the foot of the cross." So it is. None of us stands any higher. But thanks be to God, none of us need sink any lower. Thanks be to God, Christ died for me.

THE SOCIAL GOSPEL
(Gal. 3:23-26)

Imagine you are in a wheelchair, and you go to a place of business to apply for a job, or you go to a rental agency to apply for an apartment. How do you think you would be treated? Personnel at NBC News wanted to find out, so they recruited two men in wheelchairs and sent them job hunting and apartment hunting in the Washington, D.C. area. Would you be shocked to learn that they were discriminated against more than 50 percent of the time?

In most instances, the discrimination was not overt. Usually, they were treated courteously. Some people smiled and wished them well. But often the man in the wheelchair didn't even get a job interview, while another man who walked in off the street got interviews and job offers, even though he had less experience. The same thing happened in looking for an apartment. The man in the wheelchair was given excuses and told no apartments were available, while the man who walked in on his own was offered his choice of apartments. It happened repeatedly

Discrimination happens. Even after the Americans with Disabilities Act (ADA) became law, many people still have not gotten the message. It is illegal to discriminate against people with disabilities. Yet, some public buildings are still inaccessible to persons in wheelchairs. Steps or narrow doorways are obstacles that prevent disabled persons from going in. But the biggest obstacles to disabled persons are the attitudes and prejudices that lead to discrimination. Instead of assuming that all people are equal, too often we judge people by how they look. Someone in a wheelchair, of a different race or color, of a different socioeconomic class, of a different age, of a different gender—there are all kinds of people we might discriminate against.

According to the Bible, such discrimination is wrong. When Paul wrote, "there is no longer Jew or Greek, slave or free, male or female," he was saying that distinctions of race or class or gender don't matter when it comes to how we are to treat other people. When we see other people the way God sees them, we recognize that every person is precious in God's sight. We live in the most egalitarian society on earth, yet discrimination is still an ugly facet of American life. As bad as things are for persons with disabilities, there is even more discrimination along racial lines. To be sure, black-white relations in this country are better than they used to be, but there is still great suspicion and distrust and prejudice among persons of different races.

Racial segregation and discrimination are nothing new. There was enormous racial segregation and discrimination in biblical times. Jews did not mix with Gentiles. There was tremendous controversy in the Jerusalem church over whether Gentiles could become Christians. The church was also troubled with what to do with slaves who converted to Christianity. The idea of treating slaves as equals was nothing short of revolutionary. And treating women as equals was more revolutionary still. But that is precisely what Paul was advocating. In Christ, there is neither Jew nor Greek, neither slave nor free, neither male nor female. Racial, class, and gender distinctions don't matter. We are all on the same level in God's sight.

William Wilberforce was born into a very class-conscious society in 18th-century England. He came from a wealthy and privileged family, was educated at Cambridge, and then was elected to Parliament at the age of 21. During his youth, Wilberforce had been exposed to the preaching of the evangelical ex-slavetrader, John Newton, but it was as a young man that Wilberforce began to think seriously about his own spiritual condition.

Several years after he was first elected to Parliament, Wilberforce began to read the Bible. On the basis of his study and his conversations with some committed Christians, Wilberforce began to question the values upon which his life had been based: wealth, privilege, and political power. It took months of agonizing soul-searching, but eventually Wilberforce had what we might call a "conversion experience." He recognized that his life had been based on false values, so he considered resigning from Parliament and withdrawing from public life. He turned to the preacher of his youth for advice. John Newton told him, "The Lord has raised you up for the good of his church and for the good of the nation." Wilberforce began to consider how he could serve God through his political career. In the process, he discovered what would become his life's mission: to work toward the abolition of slavery.

Slave trade in the 18th century was a cornerstone of the British economy. British ships transported as many as 50,000 African slaves a year across the Atlantic Ocean. Political leaders saw the slave trade as a key factor in the nation's commercial and naval strength. Africans were either kidnapped or purchased from professional slavetraders in West Africa and loaded, manacled together, into the cargo holds of ships. A ship of 150 tons could carry 300 to 600 slaves, depending on whether they were "loose packed" or "tight packed." At least a quarter of the slaves died during the passage, many from dysentery. Sometimes an African taken up on deck and released from chains for exercise would leap into the sea, preferring to drown rather than to remain a slave. Most people in England had no idea how ugly the slave trade was. Some even used the Bible to defend slavery. It was a profitable business. Liverpool traders, for example, routinely netted a 30 percent profit by transporting slaves to the West Indies. Some argued that if Britain withdrew from the slave trade, rival nations would take up the slack, and Britain's naval power would decline.

William Wilberforce, acting on his Christian convictions, believed slavery was morally wrong. And he devoted his political career to its abolition. It was not an easy campaign. Powerful vested interests did everything they could to maintain the status quo. Planters, businessmen, ship owners, and many members of Parliament opposed the abolition of the slave trade. Year after year, Wilberforce introduced motions in Parliament, only to have them defeated. As his abolition movement gained momentum, so did the opposition. His character was often slandered. In the election of 1807, an opponent spent the astonishing sum of 200,000 pounds to try to get Wilberforce defeated. But that year, after 20 years of struggle, Parliament finally abolished the slave trade. However, it would be another 25 years before all slaves were emancipated in the British Empire.

Although Wilberforce was doggedly committed to gaining freedom for slaves, that was not his only issue. In 1804 he helped found the British and Foreign Bible Society and the Church Missionary Society. In 1813 he helped pass a law that permitted missionaries to go to India. On the local front, Wilberforce became an advocate for the "climbing boys," young chimney sweeps who were forced to work under deplorable conditions. He also took up the cause of single mothers. He established Sunday schools and orphanages for the children of parents in prison. At one time, Wilberforce supported 69 different philanthropic causes. He regularly gave away a fourth of his income to the poor, including providing an annual annuity to the widow of Charles Wesley for more than 30 years. And Wilberforce did all this with great physical limitations.

Frail and slight in stature, Wilberforce suffered from poor eyesight, chronic colitis, and a weak spine. For many years, his body had to be held upright by a crude metal frame. Because of his disabilities, Wilberforce became dependent on small doses of opium, the only effective pain killer and treatment for colitis at the time. He suffered the side effects of long-term opium use—depression, listlessness, and amnesia. In his journals Wilberforce wrote anguished prayers, asking God to deliver him from his torment. And late in his life, Wilberforce suffered personal tragedy in the untimely death of his second daughter, and financial ruin due to the mismanagement of his eldest son. Yet, through all of this, William Wilberforce remained committed to his social causes. He drew strength from reading the Bible and from spending time in prayer. On July 26, 1833, Parliament at last passed the Emancipation Bill, freeing all slaves in the British Dominions. Three days later, his life's work finally finished, William Wilberforce died. His body was laid to rest in Westminster Abbey.[1]

William Wilberforce understood that the gospel has social implications. Following the model of Jesus, Wilberforce cared about saving people, not just saving their souls. He was committed to telling people about Jesus, but he also was committed to making their lives better. For Wilberforce, faith was more than personal piety: it was putting faith into action through deeds of love.

Another committed Christian who put personal faith into action was Mother Theresa, who devoted her life to caring for the poorest of the poor. Like Wilberforce, she was a person small in stature but great in faith. Her mission was to care for the dying, the abandoned, and the outcast. She began by teaching slum children in Calcutta, India. One day she came upon a dying woman lying in the street. Mother Theresa sat with her, gently stroking her head, until the woman died. From that moment, Mother Theresa knew her calling was to minister to the "unwanted, unloved, and uncared for." She gathered about her a small group of Christian women and formed the Missionary Sisters of Charity. She and her nuns rescued dying people from the gutters and took them to their clinic to die in peace. In 1964, after Pope Paul VI gave her a white Lincoln Continental limousine that he had used during a visit, she sold it, using the proceeds to start a leper colony. Today her sisters minister to poor people in some 126 countries. They serve AIDS victims, battered women, drug addicts, and countless others the world has rejected. Mother Theresa understood that the gospel has social implications.

A Mother Theresa or a William Wilberforce comes along all too rarely, but Christ calls every Christian to serve others in his name. Christ calls every one of us to look beyond outward appearances and see all people for who they are—precious children of God. It doesn't take great stature or extraordinary abilities. All it takes is a heart of love. If God could use a tiny shrimp of a man like William Wilberforce, or a frail wisp of a woman like Mother Theresa, God can use us too.

CREATED EQUAL
(Gal. 3:26-28)

Sex discrimination still exists. The golf course is one bastion of male superiority. My wife Linda and our friend Leslie were on the golf course one day. They were playing behind a group of four men. Linda and Leslie were standing on one of the tee boxes waiting for the group ahead of them to move out of range. A man from another foursome came over and asked them, "Are you ladies waiting for something?" The obvious implication was, "Why don't you dumb women get out of our way and stop holding us up?" Leslie politely replied, "We're waiting for those men to move on so we can tee off." The man sheepishly apologized, "Sorry, I didn't see them." Then he slunk back to his own group. But Linda and Leslie were steaming. Because they were women, the man automatically assumed they didn't know what they were doing on the golf course. When I heard about this situation, it made me mad too.

Sexism is alive and well, not only on the golf course, but also in the classroom, in the office, and even in the church. Despite all the advances women have made, they are still discriminated against. Look at the administrations of most universities, the heads of most major corporations, the leaders in Congress and the other branches of government. There are a few exceptions, but overwhelmingly, men are in charge. In many industries, women earn less than men for comparable work. Studies have shown that many teachers will give a higher grade to an essay with a male name on it than to an identical essay with a female name on it. And it many churches, it's no different. It is difficult for women to assume leadership positions or even to be treated as equals.

For example, the two largest Christian denominations in the United States—the Roman Catholic Church and the Southern Baptist Convention—have no female ministers who serve as church pastors. In 1985, during a trip to the Netherlands, Pope John Paul II was asked why there are no women leaders in the Catholic Church. He replied, "because no women were present at the Last Supper either." With all due respect, that reasoning has as many holes as a slice of Swiss cheese. So, what if there were only men at the Last Supper? There were also only Jews at the Last Supper. Does that mean that only Jews can have places of leadership in the church?

It is true that Jesus chose 12 men to be his disciples. Judaism was a male-dominated culture. All societies were dominated by men at that time, just as most societies are dominated by men today. But beyond social norms, why did Jesus choose 12 men? Was he trying to show that men are superior to women? I think not! Jesus chose 12 men for symbolic purposes. Why 12, instead of 11 or 13? Because there were 12 tribes in Israel. Why men? Because the 12 tribes were descendants of the 12 sons of Jacob. The 12 disciples were chosen to represent the New Israel, the new family of God. And in this new family, the rite of entry is not circumcision, but baptism. The qualifications for admittance are not race or gender, but faith. We remember the 12 disciples, but Jesus had many more disciples beyond the 12.

Among his disciples were women. This was unheard of in Jesus' day. Against all the social norms, Jesus regularly socialized with women. Some of his best friends were women—Mary Magdalene, and the two sisters of Bethany, Mary and Martha. It was women who first were made aware of the Resurrection. It was women who were entrusted to tell the male disciples that Jesus had been raised from the dead.

Not only did Jesus treat women as equals, but the early church also began to treat women as equals. In the early church, some women assumed leadership roles. Several churches met in the homes of women, and generally the person who hosted the meetings was the leader of the church. Some of those women included Mary, Lydia, Priscilla, Chloe, and Nympha. There were also women preachers in the early church. Philip the evangelist had four daughters who prophesied. Some women in the Corinthian church also prophesied. Paul mentioned women who were co-workers with him in the Christian movement—Priscilla, Mary, Junia, Tryphaena and Tryphosa, Euodia and Syntyche. In Romans 16:1, Paul identified Phoebe as a "deacon in the church at Cenchreae." Without question, some women were leaders in the early church.

What makes this so amazing is that the biblical culture was male-dominated. For women to be treated as equals was revolutionary. For women to assume leadership roles was almost unthinkable. But it happened. What makes it even more amazing is that we even know about these women church leaders. After all, the Bible was written by men who lived in a male-dominated culture. You would expect such men to downplay the role of women or even fail to record the names of those women who were church leaders. But the men did record these names. And so, we know that women taught and preached and served as deacons and hosted church meetings and worked side by side with men in spreading the gospel.

Unfortunately, the atmosphere of equality did not last very long. In some of the early churches, treating women as equals caused problems, both in the church and in the home. That's probably why Paul in some of his letters tried to restore order by referring to the common practice of male leadership. But Paul also wrote about mutual submission, not just female submission. He wrote about husbands and wives submitting to each other out of their love for Christ (Eph. 5:21). At one point in his Corinthian correspondence, Paul counseled some women in Corinth to keep quiet in church meetings. Probably he was addressing a particular problem in a particular church situation. Earlier in the same letter, Paul assumed that women would speak and pray aloud in church. But he asked them to keep their heads covered when they did so as not to offend the customary sensibilities of the time.

Those who defend the subjugation of women based on one or two isolated scripture verses ignore the larger picture in the Bible. We must be careful not to take a temporary instruction addressed to a specific situation and make it a universal principle. For example, there was the instruction that women were to keep their heads covered in church. Today we recognize that as a temporary commandment appropriate only to that culture, not as an eternal principle mandated for all time. In another place, women were advised not to wear gold jewelry or pearls to church. Does that mean we are supposed to inspect every woman at the door today to make sure they are properly accessorized? Obviously, that too was a limited instruction intended for a particular situation. As we interpret the Bible, temporary instructions must not be turned into universal principles. Yet, there are some universal principles in the Bible.

In Galatians 3, not only are women and men labeled as equal, but in Christ all Christians are equal. In Christ there is neither male nor female, Jew nor Gentile, slave nor free. That's not to say we are all exactly the same. Obviously, there are gender differences among us, just as there are racial differences among us. We are not all exactly the same, but in the Christian community we are all equal. The universal principle is the equality of male and female. Unfortunately, most cultures still favor male domination.

We know from church history that, despite the leadership of women in the early church, it was not long before some male church leaders put women back in their place. By the middle of the second century, some churches were segregating women from men, just as they did in the synagogue. By the third century, some church fathers such as Irenaeus and Tertullian were actively discouraging women from taking leadership roles. In the following centuries men became more and more dominant in the church. And so, for most of the church's history, as for most of human history, men have been in charge.

Sadly, the church has more often been a reflection of human culture than of the spirit of Christ. Even today, there are those who use the Bible (I would say "misuse" the Bible) to keep women in submission. They ignore the universal principles and instead construe specific localized teachings to be applicable for every generation. They ignore the love of Christ and instead institute a new legalism based on male superiority. How can we possibly love our neighbors as we love ourselves unless we treat those neighbors as equals to ourselves?

As of now, women are still held back by old stereotypes and prejudices. As Christians, it is our calling to change this situation. The first step is to allow the Holy Spirit to change us. Then we can see all persons as created in the image of God. Then we will value the gifts God has given to both women and men for Christian service. Then we can see past gender, race, and every other external difference and recognize that every person is precious in the sight of God. It's not just the liberation of women we're after; it's the liberation of all of us by the Spirit of Christ. May his love make us free, and equal, even today.

QUESTIONS FOR DISCUSSION/REFLECTION

1. What did Paul mean when he said we are "all God's children"?
2. Some people say there are male and female roles in the church. Do you agree? Why or why not?

3. Why are so many churches still racially segregated?
4. What are the implications of Paul saying there is "neither slave nor free"?
5. What can churches do today to make reparations for the inequalities of the past?

NOTE

[1]This story comes from "William Wilberforce and the Abolition of the Slave Trade," *Christian History*, vol. 16, 53:1.

CHAPTER 9

CHRISTIAN FREEDOM
(Gal. 5:1-14)

Christ has set us free for freedom. Therefore, stand firm and don't submit to the bondage of slavery again. Don't let this freedom be an opportunity to indulge your selfish impulses, but serve each other through love. All the Law has been fulfilled in a single statement: Love your neighbor as yourself.

(Gal. 5:1, 13b-14 CEB)

Freedom and responsibility: the two go hand in hand. Christ has set us free! The bondage of legalism is broken. We are free to think, to believe, to speak, and to act according to the dictates of our consciences. And our consciences are shaped by our faith in Christ. No human has ultimate authority over us. As my late friend James Dunn used to say, "Ain't nobody but Jesus going to tell me what to do!"

We have freedom in Christ. Paul's only condition is that we not misuse our freedom as an opportunity to indulge our selfish impulses. Rather, we are to use our freedom to serve one another through love. Paul summed up the Law, as Jesus did in Matthew 22:39, by quoting from Leviticus 19:18, "Love your neighbor as yourself."

When Paul wrote his letter to the Galatian churches of Asia Minor, he was concerned that Jewish zealots were jeopardizing their freedom in Christ. These zealots, or Judaizers, were insisting that the Gentile Galatians must become Jews before they could become Christians. Paul strongly denounced those zealots as troublemakers who sought to deprive the Galatians of their religious liberty. Paul argued that faith in Christ, not adherence to the Jewish law, is the only way of salvation. True freedom is a gift of grace that we receive by faith.

FREEDOM IN CHRIST
(Gal. 5:1, 13-14)

We learned a new word a few years ago: "Brexit." It means the exit of Great Britain from the European Union. The financial markets didn't like that new word. Stocks immediately fell around the world due to the economic uncertainties of Brexit. Most of the markets later bounced back, but no one is sure exactly how it will all turn out. But after a popular vote, the results of the referendum meant that the United Kingdom declared independence from the EU. Apparently, a majority of people in the UK want to be free from the restrictions and obligations of union with other European countries.

Freedom is a good thing. On the 4th of July in 1776, the American colonies declared our own exit from the British empire. It was not a "Brexit," but a "US-exit" from the restrictions and obligations of union with Great Britain. Generally, freedom is a good thing. But freedom can be misused.

In Galatians, Paul celebrates our freedom in Christ. As Christians we are free from the restrictions and obligations of the Jewish religion, and from "religion" in general. This does not mean that we reject religion altogether. After all, the Jewish Bible is our Old Testament. But our freedom in Christ means that we are saved, not by religion or adherence to the Jewish law, but by faith in Jesus.

So, we are free in Christ. But freedom comes with responsibility. Freedom without responsibility can be misused. (Ask any parent of a teenager about the misuse of freedom.) Paul wrote, "For you were called to freedom, brothers and sisters, only do not use your freedom as an opportunity for self-indulgence, but through love become slaves to one another" (Gal. 5:13 NRSV). In other words, God has given us freedom, but we have the responsibility to use that freedom for the benefit of others, and not just for ourselves. Freedom without responsibility can be misused.

For example, we have great freedom in the United States in the right to bear arms. This freedom is protected by the 2nd Amendment to our Constitution, and we exercise it widely. According to the Switzerland-based Small Arms Survey, American civilians own 393 million guns. That's more than the population of the U.S. In comparison, in Australia there are about 15 guns for every 100 people. The question is: What are Americans doing with their freedom to bear arms? We may ask: Are all the guns making our country safer and more secure?

According to the 2021 Global Peace Index, terrorism, war, crime, and political instability are making many countries less peaceful. The most violent countries are Afghanistan, Yemen, and Syria. The most peaceful ones are Iceland, New Zealand, and Denmark. Out of 163 countries on the list, with Iceland the most peaceful and Afghanistan the least peaceful, the U.S. ranks number 122—which means that 121 countries are more peaceful (and less violent) than the United States. We have great freedom to bear arms, but are we using that freedom responsibly?

The number of "active shooter" incidents in the United States has risen dramatically in recent years. The shocking massacre at the nightclub in Orlando in 2016 was the deadliest mass shooting in U.S. history (up to that point). Tragically, it was not a rare event. According to data from the FBI, public shootings have become a grim new reality in American life. An "active shooter" event is defined as an individual trying to shoot and kill people in a populated area. In the year 2000 there was one such "active shooter" event. In 2015 there were 20. That equals about one active shooting incident every 18 days. Not every active shooter event leads to a massacre. Sometimes only a few people are injured or killed. But in recent years, there has been one massacre after another. Here are some grim statistics:

- 32 people killed on the campus of Virginia Tech University
- 27 people, including 20 children, killed at a Newtown, Connecticut, elementary school
- 49 people killed in a gay nightclub in Orlando, Florida
- 23 people killed at a Walmart in El Paso, Texas
- 60 people killed and hundreds more wounded at a Las Vegas, Nevada, music festival

In addition, on June 29, 2021, the *New York Times* reported there were at least 16 mass murders during the first half of 2021, including shootings in San Jose, California; Boulder, Colorado; Indianapolis, Indiana; and Atlanta, Georgia.

We have the freedom to bear arms, but are we using our freedom responsibly? More people in America are killed by guns than die in traffic accidents. The *Washington Post* on March 23, 2021 reported: "Shootings never stopped during the pandemic: 2020 was the deadliest gun violence year in decades." More than 44,000 Americans were killed by firearms in 2020. That number included some 20,000 homicides and 24,000 who died by suicide with a gun. Freedom is a good thing, but freedom without responsibility can be misused. Someone has said, "just because you have the right to do something doesn't mean it's the right thing to do."

My point here is not to dwell on gun control. I tried preaching about that some years ago and a couple of very faithful members of our church did not like it. They told me that if I preached about gun control again, they were going to leave the church. I realize this is one of many hot-button issues over which Christians disagree. That's because we have freedom in Christ. We have freedom to make up our own minds about the issues of the day. But freedom without responsibility can be misused.

Paul wrote, "Do not use your freedom as an opportunity for self-indulgence, but through love become slaves to one another" (NRSV). Earlier Paul wrote, "For freedom Christ has set us free. Stand firm, therefore, and do not submit again to a yoke of slavery" (Gal. 5:1 NRSV). Paul's words sound contradictory: do not submit again to a yoke of slavery, and, through love become slaves to one another. The difference is freedom. Through our freedom in Christ, we are no longer slaves to sin and the evil of this world. But through our freedom in Christ, we choose to become slaves to one another out of love.

What does it mean to become slaves to one another out of love? Paul wrote, "The whole law is summed up in a single commandment, 'you shall love your neighbor as yourself.'" Loving our neighbors as we love ourselves equates to becoming slaves to one another out of love.

As Christians, we love our neighbors as we love ourselves, not because we have to, but because we want to. God does not force us to do anything. God has given us genuine freedom to make our own choices and to decide how we will live. But as Christians, our freedom comes with responsibility—the responsibility to love one another. God will not make us love one another. We choose to love one another simply because we love Jesus. We choose to love one another because we remember that Jesus gave himself for us, out of love. Freedom in Christ means the freedom to love.

Oti Bunaciu grew up in Romania under communist rule, with very little freedom. The Secret Police spied on citizens they considered possible threats. They had files on Oti and his parents. Every person was required to carry an identification card. The police could stop anyone on the street and demand to see their ID card. If the police wanted to arrest you, all they had to do was confiscate your card, and you were de facto in violation of the law and could be thrown into jail. Because Oti was a Baptist, he was prohibited from pursuing certain courses of study at the university. He could not train to become a teacher because he might try to teach others about his religious beliefs. So, Oti studied engineering, because the authorities did not see that as a threat for spreading religious propaganda.

To study theology and prepare for the ministry, Oti had to leave Romania, so he went to England on a tourist visa and stayed there for three years. He was unable to return home because he would not have been allowed to leave. Only after the fall of communism was Oti able to return to his family in Bucharest. Oti had trained to become an engineer, but he felt called to Christian ministry. Oti chose to follow God's calling and became a pastor and professor of theology. And out of love for his neighbors, he founded a ministry to Romany children that became the Ruth School in Bucharest. Oti moved outside his comfort zone to minister to illiterate Roma street children because freedom in Christ means that we love our neighbors as we love ourselves.

In some respects, freedom can be a dangerous thing. Freedom can be dangerous because no one is telling us what to do. We make our own choices, and we follow the dictates of our hearts. Freedom without responsibility can lead to self-indulgence and disregard for others. But God did not create us to be puppets. God created us in his own image, and that means we have genuine freedom. God gave us minds to think our own thoughts, and experiences to help us to learn and to grow. That's why Christians don't always agree on the critical issues of our time. There are a host of issues on which Christians disagree—gun control, war, capital punishment, immigration, abortion, divorce, the role of women, the role of men, same-sex relationships, the use of alcohol and other substances, and I haven't even mentioned politics. But as Christians, we don't have to agree on every single issue. All we have to do is agree to love—to love God, and to love our neighbors as we love ourselves. The greatest freedom is to love.

JOHN LELAND: FREEDOM PREACHER
(Gal. 5:1)

Hail, fair citizens! Well thee met! Allow me to introduce myself. I am but a poor Baptist preacher: John Leland is my name. I have come to bid you stay the course on the path of liberty.

I was born on a farm in the colony of Massachusetts, near the village of Grafton, in the year of our Lord 1754. My parents were devout, religious folk, members of the Congregational Church. Today, you might call them "Puritans." At an early age, I was apprenticed to a cobbler in the town of Hopkinton, and I spent the days of my youth learning to make and to mend shoes.

One day a comely young lass named Sallie Devine came into our shop with a pair of shoes to be mended. She was, as her name implies, "divine." Wanting to prove my worthiness, I soon began to accompany her to the church of her family, a Baptist congregation meeting there in Hopkinton. The Baptists did not have such a good reputation in Massachusetts in those days. In fact, the pastor of that flock, Preacher Everett Jones, had been severely whipped for preaching the gospel without the permission of the local magistrate.

But impressed by the power of his message and by the sincerity of his conviction, soon I was persuaded to profess my own personal faith in our Lord Jesus Christ. At the age of 18 I was baptized by immersion as a believer, as is the practice of Baptists even to this day. Within two years I had become convinced that God was calling me to become a Baptist preacher too.

As I said, life was not easy there for the Baptists in Massachusetts. Our Puritan forebears had come to the New World in search of religious freedom, but once they got here, they soon became just as intolerant as the state church they had fled in England. Indeed, they made Puritanism the state church of the colony. Dissenters were not treated kindly.

A century before I was born, in 1651, a certain John Clarke, a Baptist pastor from Rhode Island Colony, was arrested and put on trial in Boston. Another Baptist preacher, Obadiah Holmes, was publicly and brutally whipped for his religious beliefs, but he kept right on preaching even during the flogging. In 1657 another Baptist, Henry Dunster, the first president of Harvard College, no less, was brought to court for opposing infant baptism. In 1666 Baptist preacher Thomas Goold was fined by the Massachusetts court for holding unauthorized religious meetings. That same Thomas Goold was banished from the colony two years later, but to his credit, he refused to leave. In 1680 the doors of the First Baptist Church of Boston were nailed shut by court order. So, you can see it was not easy being a Baptist in Massachusetts in those days.

But rather than submit, those Baptists began to press even more for religious freedom, not just for themselves, but for everyone. There was a Baptist preacher in Massachusetts, 30 years my senior, a rugged old cuss named Isaac Backus, who rode all over New England agitating for religious liberty. If that weren't enough, Brother Isaac was down there in Philadelphia during the First Continental Congress, urging the delegation from Massachusetts (and anyone else who would listen) for a guarantee of absolute religious liberty. I was just a boy at the time when Brother Isaac was traveling all over, but he blazed the trail for Baptists, and Quakers, and Jews, and all other persecuted religious groups. But let me get back to my story.

Sallie and I left our beloved Massachusetts in 1776, a year that should ring a bell with most of you (no pun intended). We moved to Virginia to help start a Baptist church. You might say we jumped out of the frying pan into the fire! You see, Baptists were not welcome in Virginia either. The Puritans weren't the problem in Virginia. The state church down there was Anglicans. I think you call those folks "Episcopalians" today. Well, those Anglicans had a stranglehold on the governments of Virginia and the Carolinas. And anyone who wasn't an Anglican suffered for it. Around the late 1760s, shortly before Sallie and I arrived in Virginia, the Anglicans got downright nasty toward the Baptists. You can understand why.

First of all, the Baptists refused to have their babies baptized, on the grounds that baptism is for believers only and church membership should be an entirely volunteer matter. Secondly, the Baptists were growing like wildfire. In 1754, the year I was born, there were only five Baptist churches with less than 100 members in the whole colony. Within 30 years, there were 205 Baptist churches in Virginia, with more than 20,000 members.

Well, that growth did not go unnoticed by the Anglican church, nor unpunished by the magistrates. In the late 1760s five Virginia Baptist pastors were thrown into jail for "disturbing the peace." In 1771 four more Baptist ministers were tried in Middlesex County for preaching outside the state church. In 1772 two more Baptists were tried in Caroline County for having preaching in their homes, and another Baptist preacher was hauled into court in Culpeper County. A year later a Baptist pastor preached from a jail cell in Chesterfield, Virginia. All told, more than 40 Baptist preachers were arrested in those years before Sallie and I came to Virginia. And that doesn't include the many other Baptists who were beaten or whipped or fined or had their property confiscated.

Call us foolhardy, but Sallie and I went down to Virginia to join our fellow Baptists in the struggle for religious freedom. Sallie was with me in this 100 percent. One time she saved my life by grabbing the arm of a man who wanted to cut me down with a sword while I was preaching. Sallie understood when I spent most of the war years on the road, traveling around Virginia on horseback and on foot, spreading the gospel and speaking out for religious liberty. We had a nice little farmhouse under some great oak trees on the Fredericksburg road, down in Orange County, Virginia. I served as pastor of churches in Mt. Poney, Orange, and Louisa. I never had the formal training the Anglican clergy had. I guess you would say I was a self-educated man, but I loved my Bible and I read everything I could get my hands on to help me better understand.

One day I got into a debate with an Anglican clergyman about state support for religion. He was for it; I was against it. It just didn't seem right to me for tax money to go to pay the salaries of certain preachers. The way I look at it, if religion is worth anything at all, people ought to be willing to support it voluntarily. If they won't freely give to it, it's not worth their support.

Well, the Anglicans didn't see it that way. They were used to taking public tax monies to fill church coffers. Anyway, one day this Anglican priest said to me, "The minister should get tax support, so he won't have such a hard time preparing his sermons." I told him that I was just a poor Baptist preacher, but I could "expound the Scriptures without any special preparation." He said, "Let's see if you can. What, for instance, would you do with Numbers 22:21, which reads, 'And Balaam…saddled his ass?'" I gave him a sermon right there, with three points:

1. Balaam, as a false prophet, represents a state-hired clergy.
2. The saddle represents the enormous tax burden of their salaries.
3. The dumb ass represents the people who bear such a tax burden.

I don't want to be a name-dropper, but I became fairly well known in those parts during the years I lived in Virginia. I got to know some pretty important men on a first-name basis—for example, Patrick Henry, Thomas Jefferson, and James Madison. I still spent most of my time preaching, but even after the war was over and we won our independence from the British, the fight for religious liberty wasn't won yet—not by a long shot.

Those Anglicans were still trying to hang on to their piece of the pie as the state church of Virginia. In 1784 they came up with a cockamamie bill that would have levied a religious tax on everyone, with the proceeds to be distributed proportionately to each denomination in Virginia. I don't care how you slice it, that's still state support for religion. I got the Baptists all riled up against it, and we got Thomas Jefferson on our side and defeated it in 1786. Finally, we had genuine religious freedom in Virginia.

But there was a bigger battle to be fought. My neighbor and friend James Madison went up to Philadelphia to help draft the new Constitution. I told him from the get-go that we Baptists wanted religious liberty guaranteed in the Constitution. Well, for whatever reason, it didn't get in there. Quite frankly, we Baptists were shocked that the Constitution said nothing about religious liberty. There was an article (Number VI) about no religious test required as a qualification for public office, but nothing to guarantee religious freedom and the separation of church and state.

So, I let it be known that I would oppose the ratification of the Constitution unless they added a Bill of Rights, with freedom of religion right up front. I wrote a letter to George Washington, expressing my concerns. I told him, and I quote: "When the Constitution made its first appearance in Virginia, we had unusual strugglings of mind, fearing that the liberty of conscience, dearer to us than property or life, was not sufficiently secured." Later, I wrote a treatise called, "Objections to the Constitution," and circulated it.

Coming back from Philadelphia after the Constitutional Convention, James Madison stopped by Mount Vernon to see the Washingtons, George and Martha. Then he came on to Fredericksburg and got wind of my opposition. Madison made a beeline for my family's place with a copy of my treatise in his pocket. After the pleasantries, Sallie and the kids left us alone, and James and I went out into the garden to hash out our differences. I told James that I had a mind to oppose his candidacy for the ratification convention in Virginia. In fact, I had a mind to run for the convention myself. James wanted desperately to be a delegate to make sure the Constitution got ratified, because he had written most of it. He asked me if there was any way he could win my support. "Only one way," I said, "and that is to give your personal promise that a Bill of Rights will be added to the Constitution as soon as it is ratified." James agreed, and the deal was done.

I threw my support behind him; he got elected; the Constitution got ratified; and sure enough, James Madison was true to his word. The Bill of Rights was added, with the First Amendment reading, "Congress shall make no law respecting an establishment of religion, or prohibiting the free exercise thereof...."

By 1791, our work in Virginia was finished. I had preached more than 3,000 sermons and baptized 1,278 converts. In 1792 Sallie and I returned to our native Massachusetts to continue the fight against state-sponsored religion there. I even served a term in the Massachusetts House of Representatives, doing what I could to promote religious freedom and the separation of church and state. Only years later, in 1833, did Massachusetts finally give up its state-sponsored church, but thank the Lord, I lived to see it! You would think that would have settled things, but I hear tell that even today you folks in this great country of ours are still having trouble keeping religion truly free, and the church and state separate. I hear tell that some modern-day "Puritans" want to organize prayers in the public schools and that "Anglicans" want tax money to go to church schools—under the guise of "educational vouchers."

Sisters and brothers, we've been down that road before, and I'm here to tell you it leads to coercion of conscience and tyranny of religion. As the apostle Paul said in Galatians 1:1, "Stand fast therefore in the liberty wherewith Christ hath made us free, and be not entangled again with the yoke of bondage." So, I'm here today to bid you to stay the course on the path of liberty. The blood of the patriots and the blood of our Lord Jesus Christ were shed for our liberty—a free church in a free state. Freedom of conscience, freedom of religion, freedom of worship: Guard it, preserve it, and cherish it. Christ died to make us free.

FREEDOM AND RESPONSIBILITY
(Gal. 5:1, 13-14)

It was only a face mask. And yet, in 2020 a simple face covering became the defining symbol of the ideological conflict between freedom and responsibility during the global Covid-19 pandemic. Along with social distancing and rigorous sanitation, face coverings were the primary defense against disease transmission. Without a vaccine to prevent infection, and with no pharmaceutical cure, the only way to slow down the spread of the illness was for people to keep their distance, wash their hands, and wear face masks. And yet, some people refused to do it, under the banner of freedom of choice.

Even the president of the United States refused to wear a face mask, despite the proclamations of his infectious disease specialists. During the first six months of the pandemic, the president was seen wearing a face mask only once. He said it was a matter of personal freedom; that people should be free to choose for themselves whether to wear a face mask or not. Tragically, many people followed the president's example. The disease continued to spread primarily because people ignored social distancing, refused to wear face masks, and refused to get the vaccine once it became available. Tragically, midway through 2021 more than 600,000 people in the United States had died of Covid-19.

Of course, freedom is important. Freedom is important to us as Americans and as Christians. Freedom is interwoven with the message of the Bible. God created humankind free. Freedom of choice was God's gift from the beginning of Creation, but along with that freedom of choice came the risk that people would misuse their freedom and turn away from God. That is exactly what happened. Adam and Eve chose to disobey God, and they lost their freedom by becoming slaves to their own selfish desires. But

God did not give up on humankind. In fact, the story of the Bible is how God has been working to make people free again. During the Exodus experience, God freed the Hebrews from bondage in Egypt. Later, God liberated the Jews from exile in Babylon. Ultimately, God provided the way through his Son for all of us to be free. Freedom is at the heart of the biblical message. Freedom was at the heart of Paul's message to the Galatians.

Paul had gone throughout Galatia preaching the gospel of freedom in Christ. His message was simple: believe in Jesus and you will be saved, you will be free. Some people didn't like Paul's message, however. Some Jewish legalists felt Paul had gone too far with this freedom business. They said there is more to it than just believing in Jesus: To be a Christian, you must first be a good Jew. You've got to keep the Torah, be circumcised, observe all the dietary laws. You've got to adhere to all the regulations of Judaism. The legalists began to follow behind Paul and undermine his message. Everywhere Paul went, they were on his tail. After Paul would leave a town, they would move in to preach a different gospel. Just believing in Jesus was not enough for them. They tried to lay upon the new Christians in Galatia a "yoke of slavery" to the Jewish law. That's why Paul wrote to the Galatians, "Christ has set us free for freedom. Therefore, stand firm and don't submit to the bondage of slavery again" (Gal. 5:1 CEB).

Paul proclaimed a radical freedom in Christ. Through our faith in Christ, we can have direct access to God. We can pray to God directly; we don't have to go through some human intermediary. We can read and interpret the Bible for ourselves. No one can dictate to us how to worship, or what to believe, or how to live. We are free to make choices for ourselves. Sometimes this doctrine is called "the priesthood of the believer." Every believer is free and equal under God.

Yet, this freedom can be misused. That's where responsibility comes in. Yes, we are free to make our own choices, but Paul cautioned the Galatians not to "let this freedom be an opportunity to indulge your selfish impulses" (Gal. 5:13 CEB). Rather, as Christians we are called to "serve each other through love." Paul reminded the Galatians that it all comes down to loving our neighbors as we love ourselves.

This is where wearing face masks during the Covid-19 pandemic came in. We were advised by the health experts to wear face masks, not only for ourselves, but also for those around us. In fact, face masks were more for the benefit of others than for ourselves. Some medical grade face masks could help protect the wearer from getting infected, but most face masks were not medical grade. The primary purpose of wearing a face mask was to inhibit infected persons from spreading the disease to others. Because the virus was largely spread through droplets expelled by coughing, sneezing, or even talking, wearing a face mask limited the droplets from infected persons reaching others. Wearing a face mask was a way of loving our neighbors as we love ourselves.

So, as Christians, we have the freedom to make choices for ourselves. But we also have the responsibility to consider how our choices affect others. We were called to freedom, sisters and brothers. Let us use this freedom to serve each other through love.

QUESTIONS FOR DISCUSSION/RELECTION

1. What does freedom in Christ mean to you?
2. What are some bondages of slavery in our time?
3. How can we avoid indulging in selfish impulses?
4. What can we do to serve each other through love?
5. How has all the Law been fulfilled in the single statement, "Love your neighbor as yourself"?

CHAPTER 10

IMITATE CHRIST
(Phil. 2:3-11)

Adopt the attitude that was in Christ Jesus: Though he was in the form of God, he did not consider being equal with God something to exploit. But he emptied himself by taking the form of a slave and by becoming like human beings.

(Phil. 2:5-7a CEB)

The Greek word *kenosis* refers to the act of emptying. Jesus emptied himself by taking the form of a slave, by becoming human. Though he was in the form of God, he did not exploit his divine nature. He humbled himself, even to the point of death. It is a powerful statement of what Christ has done for us on the cross. Paul said this is the attitude we as Christians are to adopt.

Paul wrote or quoted this "hymn" in response to the situation in Philippi. Two women in the church, Euodia and Syntyche, had been disagreeing (Phil. 4:2). Paul valued them as co-workers in the ministry of the gospel. He may have had them in mind when he wrote, "Don't do anything for selfish purposes, but with humility think of others as better than yourselves. Instead of each person watching out for their own good, watch out for what is better for others" (Phil. 2:3-4 CEB). He asked the Philippians to regard others as better than themselves, to look not to their own interests, but to the interests of each other. He told them to have the mind of Jesus, to imitate Christ.

CHRIST-MINDED
(Phil. 2:5-11)

There used to be an ad on television for a certain brand of camera. The tag line for the ad was, "Only from the mind of Minolta." The way the announcer would say those words, it sounded almost mysterious. I don't know about the camera, but the mind is a mysterious thing. Who can fathom the human mind?

The human brain is incredibly complex, comprised of 100 billion cells. And each cell has 1,000 connections with surrounding cells. This means our brains contain 100 trillion connections. And yet, the mind is more than the brain. The mind is more than 100 trillion connections, more than a mass of brain tissue and electrical impulses. The mind includes our memories, our experiences, our hopes, our dreams, our values, our beliefs, our expectations, our fears, our personality, our demeanor, our character, our faith. In other words, the mind is the essence of who we really are.

In Philippians, Paul wrote about the mind of Christ: "Let the same mind be in you that was in Christ Jesus" (2:5 NRSV). Medical science has made tremendous strides in our lifetimes. I can remember when a heart transplant was front-page news. Now, it's almost routine. Heart transplants, heart-lung transplants, kidney transplants, liver transplants … scientists are even talking about the possibility of a brain transplant someday. I cannot imagine that ever happening, but Paul talked about a mind transplant—the mind of Christ being transplanted into our minds. The more we become like Christ, the more we give ourselves to him, the more we imitate him, and the more his mind becomes a part of our personalities.

What is the mind of Christ? One word to describe it is "humility." Jesus, by virtue of his divine nature, could have come into the world as a king, a dictator, an absolute monarch. He could have lorded it over people, dominated people, ruled by power. Jesus could have expected people to wait on him, to serve him, to do his bidding. But Jesus didn't do that. He was not like the Greek gods, who according to legends, sometimes became men, but kept their divine privileges. Jesus willingly gave up his divine privileges. Even though he was in the form of God, he humbled himself, he emptied himself, he took on the role of a servant to be born in human likeness. The birth of Jesus was the American dream in reverse.

Perhaps the American dream was epitomized by Abraham Lincoln, who went from the log cabin to the White House. But the story of Jesus is just the opposite. Jesus went from the White House to the log cabin. He was in the very form of God, yet he descended to a stable in Bethlehem. But the stable, the humble birth, was not the low point. Jesus humbled himself to the level of the cross, the ultimate symbol of degradation.

The Roman philosopher Cicero, who lived shortly before Jesus, said, the cross is "the most cruel and abominable form of punishment." In Roman society, the word "cross" was an obscenity—literally a four-letter word. The Latin word for cross, *crux*, was too vulgar to be uttered in polite conversation. To understand the mind of Christ, we must look at the manger and then the cross.

Does God expect us to be like that? To be humble, to be obedient, to be a servant? It is hard for most of us to follow Jesus in that respect. By nature, we are egocentric. Our lives are centered around ourselves and getting our own needs and wants met. We naturally tend to protect our own turf, to make sure we get what's coming to us, to stick up for number one. It's hard for us to put personal ambitions on the back burner and to seek God's will first, above all else. Self-sacrifice and self-denial don't fit us very well. We judge success by other standards—achievement, money, and power.

By today's standards, Jesus was not a success at all. He never amassed wealth nor held a prestigious job. He left nothing of lasting value except the words his disciples remembered, his example of selfless service, and his ignominious death on a cross. Most of us would prefer to stop short of the stable, not to mention stopping short of the cross. But the road to life does not stop at the cross. The way of humility, service, and self-sacrifice is not a dead end. In God's eyes, by God's standards, Jesus was the ultimate success. He humbled himself, but God exalted him as our Savior and Lord. Paul continued, "Therefore God also highly exalted him and gave him the name that is above every name, so that at the name of Jesus every knee should bend, in heaven and on earth and under the earth, and every tongue should confess that Jesus Christ is Lord, to the glory of God the Father" (Phil. 2:9-11 NRSV).

Paul said if we want to live like Christians, we've got to live like Jesus. Let his mind be in us. Let his humility, love, service, and self-sacrifice be in us. That's why Jesus said if we would be his disciples, we must deny ourselves and take up our cross and follow him (Matt. 16:24). Let his mind be in you.

HE HUMBLED HIMSELF
(Phil. 2:5-11)

JoAnn was in her second month of nursing school. She prided herself on being a conscientious student, so when the first exam was scheduled, JoAnn thought she was prepared. She breezed through the test until she came to the last question. It asked, "What is the first name of the woman who cleans this building?" Surely it was some kind of a joke, JoAnn thought. She had seen the woman who cleaned the building, but she had never stopped to talk with her. How would she know her name? JoAnn turned in her exam with the last question blank. Before the class was over, another student asked the professor if the last question would count toward the test grade. "Absolutely," the professor replied. "In your careers you will meet many people. They are all significant. They deserve your attention and care."

JoAnn learned something about nursing that day, something not found in any textbook or lab assignment. She learned that all people matter. There are invisible people in most of our lives, people we see but don't really notice. The cleaning woman, the cashier at the store, the server at the restaurant, the young person, the older person, the person of a different race or nationality or social class—they all matter.

One of my former professors at Bowie State University told us about the subtle racism he had encountered as an African American. The professor was a distinguished-looking gentleman, always well-dressed, and extremely well-spoken. He had retired from the Army and earned a Ph.D. in psychology. But he related how he was often ignored in a store or restaurant, in favor of a white person. He said that no one was overtly racist toward him, but sometimes they would simply look past him, as if he weren't there.

Jesus noticed people, especially people whom others would overlook. Perhaps that was because Jesus came from a common, ordinary background himself. He was born in the most humble of circumstances. His parents were not exactly homeless, but they were sojourners with no place to lay their heads. When Jesus was born, he was laid in a feed box, because there was no room for his parents in the inn. His family was virtually invisible to the throngs of pilgrims who had come to Bethlehem. The only people who paid any notice when Jesus was born were the equally humble shepherds, whom respectable folk didn't have much use for either.

This is what Paul was getting at in his letter to the Philippians when he quoted part of a hymn. Paul said that Jesus, despite his divine nature, humbled himself and took on human form. Jesus gave up the perks and power of being equal with God and took on the frailties and limitations of human flesh. But Jesus' humility did not stop there. He emptied himself, Paul said, taking the form of a slave. As an old country preacher said, Jesus went from the penthouse to the outhouse, from the throne room of heaven to the barnyard of earth. Jesus humbled himself to take on human flesh; and he humbled himself even further to be born into a poor, common family without the means to put a proper roof over his head. John Milton, in his poem, "On the Morning of Christ's Nativity," put it like this: "He forsook the courts of everlasting day and took with us a house of darksome clay."

Not only was Jesus born into humble circumstances, but he also lived a humble life. Jesus could mix with the high and mighty, and he could be at ease with the downtrodden and lowly. Jesus was not intimidated by the intelligentsia nor impressed by the wealthy. Neither was he put off by the disreputable nor repelled by the outcasts. Even his enemies were amazed by the magnanimity of his character. They criticized him for being too open and accepting. Jesus enjoyed the company of tax collectors and sinners. He associated with people who were physically or mentally ill. He counted among his followers women and children and even former prostitutes. They were not exactly the most strategic group one might choose for starting a movement. But Jesus saw his mission as being precisely for such people. Jesus said he didn't come for the respectable people, but he came to be a servant to those whom the respectable people overlooked or even despised. Jesus came to serve the invisible people of society, the people whom no one else noticed.

The October 8, 1996 issue of *The Washington Post* carried an inspiring story about an aspiring politician named Charles Gilchrist. While serving as the county executive of Montgomery County, Maryland, he shocked the nabobs of Maryland politics when he gave up his post to become an Episcopal priest. He had a brilliant political future. Some said he might run for governor, or even for the U.S. Senate. When he announced he was leaving politics to enter seminary and study for the ministry, some of his colleagues thought he was nuts. Others thought it was a clever political ploy, while others wrote it off as a midlife crisis. But to the critics' chagrin, Gilchrist's call to the ministry was genuine.

After seminary Gilchrist moved to inner-city Chicago to direct a homeless shelter and social service agency. Later he moved to Baltimore, working with a community empowerment project to rehabilitate low-cost housing. The movers and shakers in Maryland politics couldn't get over it. Blair Lee IV, Gilchrist's former lobbyist in Annapolis, said, "I just wish he would get through his penance, take off his hair shirt, and put himself to use in government where he's got such incredible skills. He's too good to spend his time washing the feet of beggars."

Jesus was too good to spend his time washing the feet of beggars, but that is precisely what he did. He gave himself for others, even to the point of death, even death on a cross. The martyred German theologian, Dietrich Bonhoeffer, called Jesus "the man for others." Jesus lived in selfless service for other people. He came to save the world, not through power or might, but through humility and love. When Paul wrote to the Philippians about the life of Jesus, he was also writing about the Christian way of life. As Christians, we are to live the way that Jesus lived—in humility, service, and love.

Jesus set aside his own prerogatives for the sake of the people he came to save. His whole life, from the borrowed manger to the borrowed tomb, was lived in humbleness.

Jesus didn't have to live like that; he didn't have to die like that. He could have lived like a king, but he took the form of a slave. This is what makes the gospel of Jesus Christ utterly unique. It is the story of how God humbled himself out of love. In no other religion does God do that. In no other religion does God sacrifice his own Son for the sake of love. That's what makes Christianity more than just another religion. That's what makes Christianity the way to life, and life eternal.

Henri Nouwen was one of the most influential Christian writers of the 20th century. A Roman Catholic priest and a native of the Netherlands, he spent most of his life in the United States and Canada. He wrote more than 30 books, most of them on prayer and spirituality. His most famous book was *The Wounded Healer*. Nouwen taught at Notre Dame and Harvard and Yale, but he ended up as a pastor to a community in Toronto that ministered to mentally disadvantaged persons. He served there from 1985 until his death in 1996 at the age of 64.

Shortly before he died, Nouwen was speaking to a distinguished group of church leaders about his work in Toronto. He told about his friend Bill, a mentally disadvantaged man whom Nouwen had taken into his care. Bill was on stage with Nouwen, and as he was speaking, Nouwen asked Bill to come to the microphone and say something. No doubt, some of the people in the audience were thinking that they had come to hear Henri Nouwen speak, not some mentally challenged fellow. But Bill came over, and Nouwen stood beside him to give support. Bill tried to say something, but he was overcome with fear at the sight of all those people. Unable to get even a word out, Bill laid his head on Nouwen's shoulder and wept. Nouwen just stood and held his friend in his arms, as if they were the only ones there. The brilliant Dutch scholar said more about the Christian faith in that simple act of kindness than in all his books, lectures, sermons, and speeches.

That is what following Jesus is all about: standing next to one another and providing a shoulder for weeping. It's about a God who humbled himself out of love, and who calls us to love one another too.

OVERCOMING PETTINESS
(Phil. 2:3-11)

A new pastor was getting to know the members of his congregation, gradually matching up names with faces. He came to identify one woman in particular because of what she said as she greeted him after the service. The first Sunday on her way out the door, the woman grabbed the pastor's hand and shook it vigorously and said, "Pastor, you really let 'em have it today!" The next Sunday after the service, the woman said it again: "Pastor, you really let 'em have it today!" Then the third Sunday it was the same remark from the same woman, "Pastor, you really let 'em have it today!"

At first the pastor took her words as a compliment, but when she kept saying the same thing Sunday after Sunday, he wasn't so sure. Then winter came, and on a cold and snowy Sunday morning, the pastor and this woman were the only ones who made it to church. His sermon was ready, and not wanting to waste a good opportunity, the pastor preached to her. He wondered what the woman would have to say to him since she was the only one in the congregation. After the service. the woman grabbed his hand and said, "It's too bad the rest of the people weren't here, pastor, because you really let 'em have it today!"

We can be a little bit like that woman. We can see how sermons apply to other people, but when it comes to applying them to ourselves, we sometimes fail to see the connection. It's not that we claim to be perfect people. But most of us are respectable folks: we're conscientious, we try hard, and we do our best. So, when we hear a sermon about racism, most of us say, "Pastor, you really let 'em have it today!" Or when we hear a sermon about greed, we say, "Pastor, you really let 'em have it today!" When we hear a sermon about honesty, we say, "Pastor, you really let 'em have it today!" In principle, we know we are all sinners, but when it comes to getting specific about our sins, most of us gloss over our imperfections. It reminds me of the book with the title, *Yes, Lord, I Have Sinned, But I Have Several Excellent Excuses.*

Paul wrote to the Philippians about Christian living. If Paul were here, we'd probably grab his hand and say, "Paul, you really let 'em have it today!" And we would be right—at least half right. Paul did let the Philippians have it. The irony is that the Philippians were basically fine people. Of all the churches that Paul was involved with, the Philippian church may have been his favorite. He was as close to the people in Philippi as any other congregation.

Paul had begun the church by meeting with a group of godly women who used to gather down by the river for prayer. Among those godly women was a businesswoman named Lydia, a merchant who dealt in purple cloth. When Lydia heard Paul's good news about Jesus Christ, she believed and was baptized, along with the other members of her household. This was the beginning of what would become a vibrant, dynamic, joyful, generous church. On more than one occasion, when the Philippians heard that Paul was in trouble, they took up a collection and sent him a love gift of money. Clearly, these were special people, and Paul had a deep love for them. In fact, he loved them so much that he was willing to correct them.

Paul saw many good qualities in the church at Philippi—their openness, their generosity, their enthusiasm—but he also saw a potential flaw. He saw something that could pose a threat to their fellowship. He saw pettiness. Some of them could get their feelings hurt and hold a grudge. In fact, at the time when Paul wrote his letter to Philippi, two women in the church were feuding with one another. But before he singled out those two for special mention in chapter 4, Paul addressed some advice to the entire church in chapter 2. The two women, Euodia and Syntyche, had some sort of disagreement, but before he mentioned their names, he let the rest of the church know that pettiness could be a potential problem for them too.

Perhaps you remember the character from Greek mythology named Cadmus, a Phoenician prince who was on a quest to find his sister. Along the way his path was blocked by armed giants. Knowing he was not strong enough to defeat all of them in combat, Cadmus devised a plan. He hid behind a tree and threw a stone at one of the giants. Not seeing Cadmus hiding behind the tree, the giant who was struck by the stone assumed that another giant had hit him. Soon all the giants began to quarrel and take sides. They began to fight with one another until all of them were either killed or wounded. Then Cadmus came out from his hiding place and passed through their midst.

The church in Philippi was filled with potential spiritual giants, but seeds of discord sewn among the sisters and brothers threatened to disrupt their fellowship and to turn them against one another. We don't know what the issue was, but apparently it was something so minor, so inconsequential, so petty that Paul didn't consider it worth mentioning. And that's the way many disagreements are. Oftentimes they are based on some petty grievance, some minor offense that has gotten blown up out of proportion. It happens in churches, in families, in the workplace, and among friends. People acting out of petty pride take offense, and a wedge is driven into relationships.

In a letter to an advice columnist in the newspaper, a young woman who was planning her wedding wrote that she did not want any babies to attend the ceremony. But the family of the groom was upset because the groom's sister had an infant she wanted to bring. As it turned out, the sister-in-law refused to attend without her child, and she vowed never to speak to the newlyweds again. A year after the wedding, the couple was still excluded from the husband's family gatherings because of the disagreement.

Pettiness—it's a problem in families, among friends, in the workplace, and even in the church. Preaching professor Fred Craddock once said that the biggest problem in the church today is not theology, but pettiness. It's not just in the church. Among any group of people, there will be disagreements and hurt feelings. Our instinct is self-protection and self-preservation. It's not easy to hold back on our own interests and pay more attention to the interests of others. Yet, Paul asked the Philippians to be more interested in the welfare of others than in their own welfare. He asked them to be humble, and to consider others more than they considered themselves. No matter how good a Christian you are, this is hard to do. I take offense when someone insults me or ignores me. I find it hard to forgive those who hurt me, especially those who cause deliberate harm. I look after number one before I get too concerned about someone else's needs. Doing what Paul asks us to do is hard.

If all we had to go on was willpower, most of us could not live up to this high standard of Christian behavior. But we have more than sheer determination to help us. We have not only the example of Jesus Christ, but also his Spirit. The antidote to pettiness is the spirit of Christ. Jesus, who was equal with God, took on human flesh and humbled himself. Rather than sticking up for his own interests, Jesus sacrificed himself for the sake of others. Rather than seeking his own glory, he sought to give God the glory by serving others. And in the end, he endured a shameful and painful death, because he put our needs above his own needs. If you want to see a picture of the opposite of pettiness, look at Jesus. He had a magnanimity of spirit, a great and gracious heart; he answered hurt with love. This is the largeness of heart that Jesus wants for all of us. Jesus wants us to be humble, to look out for one another, to serve one another, because that is the kind of life that leads to joy.

In His Steps, the classic Christian novel by Charles Sheldon, begins with a homeless man who wanders into an affluent church and asks what it means to "follow Jesus." Before anyone can answer, the homeless man collapses before the shocked congregation.

Out of that experience, the pastor challenges his people to "do what Jesus would do" for a year. The people accept the challenge, and their lives are not the same. What would Jesus do? It's a good question to ask ourselves as we seek to follow Christ.

QUESTIONS FOR DISCUSSION/REFLECTION

1. What was the "attitude" that was in Christ Jesus?
2. What would it mean for us to "empty" ourselves?
3. How do we balance a healthy self-interest with interest for others' needs?
4. Humility is not always valued in today's society. In what ways can humility be a healthy personality trait?
5. How can we imitate Christ in our daily living?

CHAPTER 11

CLOTHE YOURSELVES WITH LOVE
(Col. 3:12-17)

> *As God's chosen ones, holy and beloved, clothe yourselves with compassion, kindness, humility, meekness, and patience. Above all, clothe yourselves with love, which binds everything together in perfect harmony.*
>
> (Col. 3:12, 14 NRSV)

The Christian life involves a new nature. It's not just about what we believe; it's about our personalities, our attitudes, and our actions. It's about what we do. Love is something you do, not just something you feel. Such love includes compassion, kindness, humility, meekness, patience, forgiveness, harmony, and peace. Such love creates community. It does not gloss over differences but resolves differences by bearing with one another and forgiving one another. Above all, as Christians we are to clothe ourselves with love.

Colossae was a town in Asia Minor, not far from Ephesus. Paul did not start the church in Colossae, but he felt a kinship with the Christians there. As in most churches, there were disagreements among them. Paul's concern was that they "lead lives worthy of the Lord" (Col. 1:10 NRSV). Paul's description of Christ in Colossians 1:15-20 is a "high Christology," meaning he places Jesus in the larger context of God's eternal purposes. Paul writes about not only the Jesus of history, but also the Christ of eternity, in whom "the fullness of God was pleased to dwell" and through whom God reconciled all things "through the blood of his cross" (vv. 19-20 NRSV).

In his various letters to churches in Rome, Corinth, Galatia, and Colossae, Paul echoed again and again the same theme: we are one in Christ. Race, ethnic background, gender, social class—none of these matter because we are one in Christ. Jews divided the world into two kinds of people: (1) Jews and (2) non-Jews (or Gentiles or Greeks). Likewise, Greeks divided the world into two kinds of people: Greeks and non-Greeks (or barbarians). Racial prejudice, stereotyping, and profiling are nothing new. But in Christ, we are one. We are one body, through the peace and love of Christ.

ONE IN THE SPIRIT
(Col. 3:12-15)

Believe it or not, people in the church do not always agree. That was the way it was in the church at Colossae, and that's the way it is in most churches today. We may be one in the Spirit, but we are not always of one mind. People of goodwill may have honest differences of opinion. Especially in a church that emphasizes democracy and freedom of speech, there will be times when we don't see eye to eye. This was the case in a Worship and Music Commission meeting I attended at my church some years ago.

We were discussing our Sunday morning worship services for the summer, and how to combine two services into one. The discussion was lively, and even a little heated at times. Voices were raised, and some things were said in a less-than-diplomatic way. I could understand why: how we worship is a sensitive issue. Plus, there were some personal dynamics involved.

Some people were tired after a full day at work. Some were hungry because they had not eaten dinner. Some were frustrated that we didn't have enough time to carefully consider all the ramifications of a blended worship service. Still others felt they were getting run over by the preferences of the more outspoken members of the commission. It was not an ugly meeting, but it was a tense one. There were some genuine disagreements. No one was in the wrong, no one was to blame, and no one was causing trouble. That's what happens when people get together to discuss something they care deeply about.

Many churches experiment with different styles of worship. For example, one local church has three different Sunday morning worship services: a traditional service, a contemporary service, and a blended service that combines elements of the traditional and the contemporary. The major differences in the services are the order, the formality, and the style of music. In our church, for 10 months out of the year, we offered two worship services every Sunday morning: a contemporary service and a traditional service. The main differences were the starting times, the order, the formality, and the music.

At the early service we sang praise and worship songs accompanied by a synthesizer. At the second service we had the music of hymns, choir, and organ. I preached basically the same sermon and used the same scripture text, although at the early service I preached from the floor level without notes, so there were some minor differences.

When the members of the Worship and Music Commission began to discuss how to blend elements of the two services into one, differing ideas were expressed. That's to be expected. We have different preferences when it comes to music. We have different expectations of what makes a meaningful worship experience. One of the blessings of our free-church tradition is the freedom we have to worship as we see fit. There is no prescribed liturgy or mandated style we must follow. We are free to make our own decisions about the way we worship. But that freedom can cause conflict. This is the point where our Christian faith is put to the test.

Talking about worship styles is a specific example of a much larger issue—namely, how we handle disagreements in all the areas of our lives. Particularly as Christians, how do we resolve differences in a way that remains true to our principles and convictions? The Bible has a definite bias in favor of unity. One basic tenet of our Christian faith is that we should learn to live together in harmony and peace. And yet, when strong personalities are involved, unity is easier said than done.

Apparently, there were some strong personalities in many of the early churches. When we read Paul's letters to the churches, we get the impression that one of the reasons he wrote was to encourage the church members to get along with one another. In a few of his letters, Paul even named names, specifically identifying some bickering church members who needed to get along. In Colossians he wrote in general terms, but the message was the same: Christ has called us to live together in harmony and peace.

Colossians 3 could very well have been written after a contentious committee meeting. In verse 13 Paul wrote, "Bear with one another and, if anyone has a complaint against another, forgive each other." Paul was not some starry-eyed optimist. He did not assume that Christians are somehow impervious to personal slights and insults. He knew very well how people can irritate us. People who are insincere or dishonest or self-centered can get on my nerves in a big way. But in the church, among Christians, we are supposed to bear with one another, and to forgive those who have done us wrong. That is hard to do. If it were a matter of willpower, most of us would fail at it. But we have more than willpower to help us. We have the presence of God's Spirit in our lives, and the fruit of God's Spirit. Paul identified some of those fruits of the Spirit: compassion, kindness, humility, meekness, patience. These fruits of the Spirit can help us to bear with one another. If we are compassionate and kind and humble and meek, and above all, patient, we can learn to look past hurt feelings to the greater good. And, the greater good is unity.

Now, unity is not the same as uniformity. Unity does not mean we agree on everything. But unity means there are times when we will put aside our own personal preferences for the larger good of the group. That principle of unity applies in a church, in a marriage, in a family, in a work environment—in any meaningful relationship. Unity is hard to achieve, and even harder to maintain.

For a brief time, the first church in Jerusalem was united around the teaching of the apostles, but that unity did not last very long. Soon the apostles were scattered all over the Mediterranean world preaching the gospel, and James the brother of Jesus became the leader of the Jerusalem church. When Paul came on the scene, he had some conflicts with James and the other leaders of the Jerusalem church. And it would be fair to say that for most of Christian history there have been various divisions within and among churches.

For a while, the church was seemingly unified under the authoritarianism of the bishop of Rome. But in reality, there have been splinter movements and larger schisms throughout Christian history. In the 11th century the Great Schism divided the church into two parts: Roman Catholic and Eastern Orthodox. Then in the 16th century the Protestant Reformation resulted in many different churches and styles of worship. Today, there are thousands of different church groups, not to mention countless divisions within individual churches.

Unity is hard to achieve, and even harder to maintain. But Jesus prayed that his disciples be one, and that God's Spirit be at work in our lives to draw us together. We may not agree on everything—in fact, we will not agree on everything—but we are called to find some common ground in our common faith.

The movie *Babe* is the story of barnyard animals who can talk. The humans in the movie never see the animals talking, but the viewers do. Yet, despite the fact that the animals can talk with each other, they don't communicate very well with each other. The reason they don't communicate well is because they have little respect for one another. The dogs think the sheep are stupid, and the sheep think the dogs are vicious. The cat thinks she is better than all the other animals because she lives in the house. And no one can see much use for the duck, except maybe as a meal for the farmer's family. But along comes Babe, a little pig who has none of the prejudice of the other animals. Babe respects everyone and sees values in all the animals. As a result, Babe is genuine and thoughtful and considerate of all the other animals. And gradually, over time, as Babe treats all the animals with respect, they begin to treat Babe with respect too.

That's what it boils down to in any harmonious relationship: respect. If we respect one another, we will treat one another the right way. That does not mean we will always agree. Sometimes we agree to disagree, and then we go on caring for one another despite our differences.

Philip Melanchthon was a colleague of Martin Luther during the Protestant Reformation. Although Luther was the visionary behind the Reformation, Melanchthon was the theologian who helped to articulate the vision. Melanchthon helped expound such crucial doctrines as the authority of Scripture, the priesthood of the believer, and justification by faith. He was the principal author of the statement of faith, *The Augsburg Confession*. Besides being a brilliant scholar, Philip Melanchthon was a peacemaker. He tried to bring Martin Luther and the other reformers together, and he even worked to build bridges of understanding with those loyal to the pope. In was Philip Melanchthon who wrote, "In necessary things, unity; in doubtful things, liberty; in all things, charity."

In things that are essential, let us be united. In things that are not essential, let us respect the freedom of others to have different opinions. In all things, let us love. Unity, liberty, charity—and the greatest of these is love.

THE PEOPLE OF GOD
(Col. 3:12-14)

He was new in the office, and he stood in front of a large paper shredder, looking confused. A secretary walked by and asked, "Need some help?" "Yes," the man replied, "how does this thing work?" "Simple," she said, "like this." Then she took the fat report from his hands and fed it into the shredder. "Thanks," he said, "but where do the copies come out?"

Some people approach the Bible with the same confusion. They start out wanting to copy the message of the Bible into their own lives, but they end up shredding to bits what the Christian faith is all about.

At first, I thought I had misread the headline. It was from an article that appeared in a religious publication about Christian ethics. The magazine was supposed to provide guidance for making ethical decisions from a Christian perspective, so I looked at the headline again and again. No, I had not misread it. The headline read, "Assault Weapons Should Be Available."

The article was written by a man who identified himself as a ruling elder in the Presbyterian church. In the article he argued that there is nothing incompatible between assault weapons and the Christian life. He said that according to the Bible, God would not want us to ban assault weapons. He cited what happened after Cain murdered Abel. God did not ban the ownership of whatever it was that Cain used to kill his brother.

He also cited some verses from the Old Testament where Israelite warriors were told to provide their own weapons. Then he appealed to Jesus, who in one verse in Luke says something about a sword. He concluded that not only is there nothing wrong with assault weapons, but that God wants us to have them! Not surprisingly, the author of the article served as executive director of an organization called Gun Owners of America. What shocked me was not just the convoluted exegesis, but the fact that a magazine about Christian ethics would publish it.

I realize that some Christians are gun owners. For those in the military or in law enforcement, guns may be a necessary part of their jobs. Some people own guns for hunting or target shooting. Some people own guns for self-defense. But there is a distinction between guns designed for hunting or target shooting and guns designed for killing people. We live in a society that is gun crazy. Almost every day in almost every city around the country innocent men, women, and children are killed with guns. I have a hard time reconciling the private ownership of assault weapons with what I read in the Bible about the way Christians are supposed to live.

In Colossians 3, Paul presents a very different picture of what Christian conduct is like. He lists some characteristics of Christian living—compassion, kindness, humility, gentleness, patience. These are not necessarily the virtues of American society. Indeed, some people might dismiss these Christian virtues as being weak and ineffective. But nothing could be further from the truth. In fact, it takes a much stronger person to be compassionate, kind, humble, gentle, and patient than to try to solve your problems with a gun. It takes a much stronger person to forgive someone who has wronged you than to seek revenge. It takes a much stronger person to put up with irritating people than to attack them or avoid them. It takes a much stronger person to be a Christian than to just go with the flow and live like everyone else.

In my mind, Jesus was the strongest person who ever lived. He didn't just talk about compassion, kindness, humility, gentleness, and patience. He really lived like that. He didn't just talk about forgiveness. He forgave those who had hurt him, even from the cross. I wonder what Jesus would say about assault rifles. The whole idea behind an assault rifle is that you can solve problems by getting rid of people. But Jesus taught a very different lesson: that we solve problems by loving people. Jesus said we are to even love our enemies. Closer to home, Jesus said that we are to love our neighbors as we love ourselves. This means we are to love our fellow church members and our family members as we love ourselves. Try loving people, especially those you don't get along with, and see what kind of strength that takes.

God calls us to love because God has chosen us to be his people. In the Old Testament, the Jews understood themselves to be God's chosen people. But in the New Testament, God's chosen people are those whom he has called in Jesus Christ. God calls all Christians to be his people, and the most important thing the people of God can do is to love. And the way we love is to be compassionate, kind, humble, gentle, patient, and forgiving. When we demonstrate these virtues, we will find ourselves bound together in love.

Giacomo Puccini wrote some of the most beautiful operas of the 20th century. But while Puccini was working on his last opera, *Turandot*, he became sick with cancer. He told his students, "If I cannot finish *Turandot*, I want you to finish it for me." Shortly after that, he died. Puccini's students did what their master had asked. They carefully studied what he had done, and then they completed his work. The world premiere of *Turandot* was presented in Milan, directed by one of Puccini's favorite students, Arturo Toscanini. The opera went beautifully until it reached the point where Puccini had been forced to stop. At that point, the performance stopped. The following night the opera was presented again. Again, the opera stopped when it reached the point where Puccini had stopped. With tears in his eyes, Toscanini turned to the audience and said, "Thus far the master wrote, but then he died." A hush fell over the opera house. Then Toscanini picked up his baton, and said, "But his disciples finished his work." And with that the opera continued. Some said it was the greatest work Puccini had ever done.

Our Master has asked us to finish what he started. But he who died is yet alive and with us still, and by his power we can do great deeds. We are the people of God. God has chosen us to continue the divine work of love.

WHERE HEALING BEGINS
(Col. 3:12-17)

Some years ago I had outpatient surgery on my head to remove skin cancer, basil cell carcinoma. The dermatologist didn't get it all. She operated on me a second time, and once again the margins did not come back clear. She sent me to a specialist who operated on my scalp yet a third time. After the third operation, there wasn't enough skin left to stitch up, so the surgeon left the wound open, to heal on its own. The good news was that after the third surgery the skin cancer was finally removed. The bad news was that the wound healed unevenly, so that every three weeks I had to go back to the surgeon for more treatment. After six months, I was ready for the healing to be done. Sometimes healing takes a long, long time.

Our country has taken a long, long time healing from the wounds of the past. Jim Wallis, founder of the Christian organization Sojourners, says that racism is America's original sin. Unlike slavery in the Bible, slavery in the American experience was based on race. One race was presumed to be superior to other races. And that presumption issued not only in slavery, but also in the genocide of Native Americans and in a history of racism that has stained our nation to this day. Slavery ended more than a century and a half ago, but the legacy of slavery continues. Native Americans were forced from their lands long ago, but the legacy of ill treatment of Native Americans continues. There also continues prejudice against immigrants, especially those from Latin America. Thank God, we are further down the road toward the healing of that ugly wound of racism, but we have a way yet to go.

The scripture passage from Colossians is about healing old wounds. It's about God's prescription for moving beyond the pains of the past. It's about the way that Christians are supposed to treat one another. It's about how we can find a way to live together in harmony and peace. If people in this country had followed this teaching from the beginning, racism never would have been such a problem in America. If the peace of Christ had ruled in the hearts of the early European colonists, Native Americans would not have been driven from their lands and Africans would not have been enslaved. If the early colonists and their descendants had clothed themselves with love, they would have treated all people with dignity and respect. But that didn't happen. Instead, European colonizers treated Native Americans and Africans as inferior beings. And our society has been wracked by racial divisions ever since.

Paul wrote in Colossians that as Christians we are God's chosen ones, holy and beloved. Sometimes Christians don't act like that, but that's who we are—holy and beloved. As such, we are to clothe ourselves with compassion, kindness, humility, meekness, patience, and love. Beyond that, we are to forgive each other, just as the Lord has forgiven us. There can be no healing from the wounds of the past without forgiveness.

Brooks Douglass was only 16 years old when his family was brutally attacked in their home in Oklahoma. His father was a respected Baptist pastor, his mother was a gifted singer, and his 12-year-old sister was the reigning Miss Teen Oklahoma. It was around dinnertime when a scruffy stranger approached their home pretending to be lost. After Brooks invited the man to come inside to use the phone, the stranger pulled a handgun from his belt, and an accomplice burst through the door with a shotgun. The two assailants, high on alcohol and cocaine, tied up Brooks and his parents, then sexually assaulted his little sister. They ransacked the house and terrorized the family for nearly three hours. Before they left, they shot Brooks, his parents, and his sister.

Though grievously wounded, Brooks and his sister survived the gunshots, but they watched their parents die. Somehow, Brooks and his sister managed to get untied and stagger to the family car. With blood pouring from their wounds, they made it to the home of a local doctor. As they fought for their lives in intensive care, the two missed their parents' funeral. They were released from the hospital three weeks later and given all of one hour to collect some of their belongings from their home before it was sold.

Brooks and his sister—emotionally devastated, shocked, grieving, and homeless—were then separated. Brooks' sister went to live with some distant relatives about an hour away. Brooks moved in a with a family from their church so he could finish his senior year of high school. The two men who had murdered his parents, raped his sister, and shot all of them in the back, eventually were caught and put on trial. In fact, there were a series of trials, and Brooks and his sister had to take the stand nine different times to tell what had happened. Even though Brooks and his sister hardly saw each other and never received counseling, law enforcement officials and prosecutors marveled at their poise giving their testimonies. Both assailants were convicted and sentenced to death.

Brooks eventually went to college, and then law school. At the age of 27 he was elected to the state Senate of Oklahoma. The town had not forgotten the horrific crimes that had been visited upon his family, and Brooks became an advocate for victims' rights. He pushed through legislation that would allow victims' families to watch a convicted murderer be put to death. Both men who had attacked his family were sentenced to death, but one of them appealed his conviction on the grounds that he was denied a court-appointed psychiatric evaluation for an insanity defense. The appeal went all the way to the U.S. Supreme Court, and despite having signed a statement acknowledging full responsibility for the killings, the murderer was granted a new trial and received life in prison.

One day in 1995, while touring the state prison as a part of his duties as a state senator, Brooks impulsively asked to meet with that particular prisoner, the man who had killed his parents but escaped the death penalty due to a legal technicality. Prison officials tried to talk him out of it, but Brooks was insistent on seeing the killer.

Surprisingly, the killer agreed to meet with him. What happened during their meeting no one could have predicted: The killer was brought shackled into the sparse room in the prison and seated at a spare wooden table. Before Brooks could say anything, the killer blurted out, "I am so sorry for what I did to your family. I wish I could do anything to take it back. The truth is I don't know why I did it. It was senseless."

Brooks was stunned. He told the killer that for the last 15 years all he wanted was for the man to be dead. Brooks told him that he had ruined his life, and ruined his sister's life, and taken away his family. But then Brooks realized that what had happened that night had controlled both of their lives. Brooks began to feel a strange compassion for the killer. Before their meeting was over, Brooks told the man that he forgave him.

A few months later, Brooks and his sister watched as the other killer was executed by lethal injection. But seeing the other man die brought Brooks and his sister no peace. The man was dead in seven minutes, without uttering any final word of apology or remorse. Brooks was glad he was gone, but there was no real closure. So, instead of running for re-election to the state Senate, Brooks joined the Army Reserves. He trained for the Special Forces, and he was deployed to the Middle East. After his military service, Brooks got married, for the third time, and ended up in California. That's when his life took an even more surprising turn.

In 2007 Brooks enrolled in a screenwriting class. Upon hearing his story, the professor encouraged Brooks to write a screenplay based on his experiences. As Brooks began to write, he unpacked memories that had been haunting him for almost 30 years. The crucial scene of the screenplay would be the meeting he had with his parents' killer in the penitentiary. That meeting would become the crux of the film's message, along with a turning point in Brooks' own life. Unexpectedly, just telling the story began to release him from the anger and rage that had consumed him all those years. Brooks realized that by forgiving the killer he could begin the process of turning his life around. He realized that forgiving the killer was what his father would have wanted him to do. But even more, forgiveness was the key to healing the wounds of the past.

The screenplay was made into a movie, *The Amendment*. Brooks insisted on playing the part of his father. In one riveting scene, Brooks preaches his father's last sermon. It is a sermon about forgiveness, about letting go of past grudges. Brooks' main purpose in making the film was to show how God had turned something horrible into something good. Brad Henry, the former governor of Oklahoma, was a friend of Brooks since his days in the state legislature. After the movie came out, Brad said of Brooks, "He's the happiest he's been since I've known him."[1]

Sadly, Brooks Douglass died in May 2020 after a six-year battle with cancer. He was only 56. But his memorial page describes his life this way: "If lifetimes were measured in miles and meaning rather than years, Brooks lived a very full life." The movie he created was "to honor his parents and tell their family's true story of love, loss, and healing after a devastating crime." As Brooks wrote for *The Amendment* movie tag line, "we are capable of more than we ever thought possible."[2]

Forgiveness is the key to healing old wounds from the past. Sometimes healing takes a long, long time. But forgiveness is the turning point for letting go of the past and moving toward a better future. We cannot undo injustices that were done; but we can clothe ourselves with compassion, kindness, humility, meekness, patience, and love. We can bear with one another, and if anyone has a complaint against another, we can forgive each other, as God has forgiven us. We can let the peace of Christ rule in our hearts.

Sometimes life is terribly unfair, and people are terribly cruel, but God is good, and his mercy endures forever. Just as the Lord has forgiven us, may we also forgive.

QUESTIONS FOR DISCUSSION/REFLECTION

1. Of the qualities God asks of us—compassion, kindness, humility, meekness, patience—which do you find to be most difficult?
2. How is it possible to forgive a grievous wrong?
3. What would it mean for you to clothe yourself with love?
4. How do we let the peace of Christ rule in our hearts?
5. How does being thankful enable us to live in a Christlike manner?

NOTES

[1] The story of Brooks Douglass comes from *Newsweek*, August 22 and 29, 2011.
[2] www.brooksdouglass.net/.

CHAPTER 12

ALL SCRIPTURE IS GOD-BREATHED
(2 Tim. 3:10-17)

All Scripture is God-breathed and is useful for teaching, rebuking, correcting and training in righteousness, so that the servant of God may be thoroughly equipped for every good work.
(2 Tim. 3:16-17 NIV)

"All scripture is inspired by God" (2 Tim. 3:16a NRSV). Of course, Paul was writing about the Old Testament. In his time, the New Testament was beginning to be written, but only several centuries later would the church decide which letters of Paul, which gospels, and which other writings would be included. Yes, the church came to believe that the 27 books of the New Testament canon were divinely inspired, but in his second letter to Timothy, the God-breathed scripture Paul was referring to was the Old Testament. Just as God breathed life into the first human being in Genesis 2:7, so God breathed life into the words of scripture that became a guide for faithful living.

Paul's point was that the Old Testament was inspired because it pointed to Jesus Christ. In 2 Timothy 3:15 Paul reminded Timothy that from childhood he had "known the sacred writings that are able to instruct you for salvation through faith in Christ Jesus" (NRSV). As a pharisee, Paul had valued the sacred writings as a guide for righteous living. As a Christian, he valued the sacred writings because they prepared the way for Jesus.

For Christians, we view the Old Testament through the lens of the New Testament. We remember how Jesus reinterpreted some sayings of the Old Testament in the Sermon on the Mount in Matthew's gospel. Jesus repeatedly told his hearers, "You have heard that it was said…but I say to you…" (Matt. 5:21-22, 27-28, 31-32, 33-34, 38-39, 43-44). Jesus went beyond a legalistic reading of the Old Testament to reinterpret the meaning. Thus, as Christians, we believe that Jesus himself is the criterion by which we interpret scripture, both Old and New Testaments. The purpose of scripture is to equip us for every good work. Yet, scripture requires interpretation. Paul encouraged Timothy in 2 Timothy 2:15 to do his best to be one who "correctly handles the word of truth" (NIV), or in other words, one who is "rightly explaining the word of truth" (NRSV).

BACK TO SCHOOL
(2 Tim. 3:10-17)

Many students go back to school at the end of summer. When I was a kid, I dreaded that time of year. I did okay in school, but I did not like it. My grandfather was the superintendent of the elementary schools in our city, so all my teachers knew me. They all expected me to be an outstanding student. That was a lot of pressure on a kid, in addition to the expectations my parents and grandparents had for me. Because of those expectations, I usually made good grades, except in handwriting. No matter how hard I tried, my handwriting was never good. In elementary school, one teacher kept me in from recess so I could practice my penmanship. It didn't help. I still got "C's" on my report cards for handwriting.

Part of my poor penmanship was due to genetics, and part was circumstantial. My father had beautiful penmanship; my mother, not so much. It's like having a good voice for singing: either you have it, or you don't. And, writing left-handed didn't help. We lefties tend to curl our hand around as we write.

The circumstantial part of my poor penmanship came from the many years I spent in school. The irony of not liking school as a kid is that I ended up going to school a lot as I grew older. I spent decades sitting in classrooms taking notes. Most of my classes were lecture format. The teacher would lecture, and the students would write down what the teacher said. If I wanted to record most of what the teacher said, I had to write fast. Even today, when I write something, I do it fast. Fast writing does not enhance legibility. I learned to write, but never to write well.

What does it take to learn, besides aptitude and motivation? In our scripture Paul wrote to his protégé Timothy. Paul was a mentor to Timothy. From the book of Acts, we learn that Timothy was the son of a Greek father and a Jewish mother who had become a Christian (Acts 16:1). His mother and grandmother had instructed Timothy in the Scriptures from his childhood, and he had become a Christian through their influence. In Acts, Timothy appears as a traveling companion of Paul and a fellow worker for the gospel. Paul mentioned Timothy in several of his letters (Romans, 1 and 2 Corinthians, Philippians, etc.).

Paul directed most of 2 Timothy specifically to Timothy as a church leader. The letter was included in the New Testament because much of what Paul wrote to Timothy could apply to the larger Christian community. Many of Paul's instructions to Timothy were for other Christians too. It's clear that Timothy had learned a lot from Paul. Yet, Paul wrote to encourage Timothy to keep learning and to keep growing as a Christian.

School is intended for learning and growing—mentally, emotionally, and socially. The question for students, and for all of us, is: How do we learn and grow? Paul's letter provides some answers.

First, we learn from example. Paul was an example to Timothy. Timothy had observed Paul firsthand. He had observed Paul's teaching, his conduct, his aim in life, his faith, his patience, his love, his steadfastness, his persecutions, his sufferings. One of the best ways we learn is from mentors and role models who are examples to us of how to live.

I have been blessed by many positive role models of Christian living. The first pastor I got to know was J.P. Allen, who served my home church in Fort Worth, Texas when I was a teenager. There were others in my church who were positive influences on me—Sunday School teachers, youth leaders, the music minister. But Dr. Allen was my role model. As a senior in high school, I was selected to be pastor during Youth Week. I didn't give a sermon, but Dr. Allen and the associate pastor, Roy DeBrand, took me under their wings. They showed me that the work of a pastor involves more than just one hour on Sunday mornings. Rev. DeBrand took me with him to make hospital visits. Dr. Allen invited me to give a prayer during the Wednesday night prayer meeting, and then to read scripture during the worship service on Sunday morning. Their encouragement helped kindle in me the idea that I could be a pastor one day.

Although Dr. Allen resigned as pastor when I was in college to accept a job with the Southern Baptist Radio and Television Commission, we stayed in touch. One summer during seminary he invited me to work as a correspondence counselor for the Commission. After I was called to my first church in Silver Spring, I invited Dr. Allen to come and give a series of sermons for a kind of renewal week. Dr. Allen maintained interest in me even after I moved to another church. One weekend I was back in Texas visiting my parents. My book, *Storytelling in Preaching*, had just been published. Dr. Allen, who had been retired for several years, was present in the congregation that Sunday morning. He came up to me after the service and told me he had read my book and was proud of me. It was one of the most meaningful affirmations I have ever received.

When I was in college, the pastor who came to my home church after Dr. Allen was also a tremendous role model. His name was John Claypool. Dr. Claypool was the one I talked with about the possibility that I was being called into the ministry. He encouraged me to come forward the following Sunday morning to declare my calling. A couple of years later, Dr. Claypool led my home church to license me to the gospel ministry. Both Dr. Allen and Dr. Claypool were role models as preachers, but they were even better role models as pastors.

So, one way that we learn is by the example of others. Timothy learned from Paul's example. I learned from the examples of Dr. J.P. Allen and Dr. John Claypool.

Motivational speaker James Wealthy says, "The only way we learn in life is by mentors, and mistakes." He has a point. We learn by mentors, by examples, by role models. But we also learn by mistakes, or more positively, from experience. We learn by doing.

During their total eclipse adventure in Wyoming in 2017, Linda and our daughter Amy spent a night sleeping on the ground in a tent. Neither of them had ever set up or slept in a tent. They tried setting up the tent on a friend's deck in Colorado before they got to Wyoming. They set it up okay, but taking it down was another matter. So, they learned from their mistakes. They decided to watch a demonstration video. Then, they tried it again. When they got to Wyoming, they had no trouble setting up the tent or taking it down, because they had learned from their experience and their mistakes. They had learned by doing.

That's the way we learn and grow as Christians. We learn from experience. Sometimes we make mistakes along the way, but we learn by doing. We act like Christians, and eventually it becomes second nature to us. We become equipped for every good work.

Beyond learning from mentors, and learning from mistakes, Paul says there is a third way we can learn: through study. Paul urged Timothy to continue to study "the sacred writings that are able to instruct you for salvation through faith in Christ Jesus" (2 Tim. 3:15). Studying the Bible is crucial for us to learn and to grow as Christians. That's why churches have Sunday School, Vacation Bible School, and Bible study groups and opportunities. Studying the Bible is essential to our understanding what the Christian life is all about. As Paul said, "All scripture is inspired by God and is useful for teaching, for reproof, for correction, and for training in righteousness" (2 Tim. 3:16).

In addition to the Bible, books written about the Bible and about Christian living can help us to learn and grow as Christians. The problem is, many of us don't read that much. Christian author Philip Yancey laments, "The death of reading is threatening the soul." In other words, many Christians are not reading as they once did. Yancey says that his office is surrounded by tall bookcases laden with 5,000 books. Over the years, as he has read those books, he has marked them and used them to inform his own writing. He says those books, to a large degree, have formed his professional and spiritual life. They have helped define who he is and have ushered him on a journey of faith. But he confesses he is reading fewer books than he used to. The Internet and social media have changed his reading habits.

Nicholas Carr, in his book, *The Shallows*, observes that most Americans, and especially younger Americans, are experiencing a precipitous decline in the amount of time spent reading. A 2016 Nielsen report calculates that the average American spends more than 10 hours a day watching television, or using computers, or other electronic devices. That means 65 percent of our waking hours we are engaged with electronic media, leaving little time for reading books.

When Warren Buffett was asked his secret to success, he pointed to a stack of books and said, "Read 500 pages like this every day. That's how knowledge works. It builds up, like compound interest." I dare say not many of us could read 500 pages a day. But if we were to spend a little less time on social media and watching television, we might find more time to read. Reading can help us to learn and to grow.

Albert Einstein said, "Once you stop learning, you start dying." Conversely, when we keep learning, we keep living. May we continue to learn. May we learn by example, by experience, and by study so that we might continue to grow as followers of Jesus Christ.

RIGHTLY DIVIDING THE WORD OF TRUTH
(2 Tim. 2:15, 3:14-17)

In his second letter to Timothy, Paul said, "Do your best to present yourself to God as one approved, a worker who does not need to be ashamed and who correctly handles the word of truth" (2 Tim. 2:15 NIV). When I arrived on the seminary campus in August of 1973, I was almost in awe. I was surrounded by hundreds of other college graduates who had been "called into the ministry." Plus, all my professors had PhDs. My feelings of inadequacy were substantial. Did I have what it takes to become a pastor? Walking around the campus, I almost felt like I was on holy ground.

The first day of classes I approached Norton Hall, a massive Georgian-architecture building containing classrooms and the administrative offices. On one end of Norton Hall was a wing of the building that housed the post office on the bottom floor and the dining hall on the second floor. Above the doors was a large stone plaque with the seminary seal surrounded by words of scripture, "Rightly dividing the word of truth." The words were a quotation from 2 Timothy 2:15, taken from the King James Version of the Bible. One modern translation phrases Paul's instructions to Timothy as "rightly explaining the word of truth" (NRSV), but the King James had it "rightly dividing the word of truth." Either way, I knew what the slogan meant. I was there at the seminary to learn how to rightly divide the word of truth. I would spend the next three and a half years preparing myself to rightly interpret the Bible.

We are people of the Book. The Bible is our authority in matters of faith and practice. The Bible is our guide when it comes to what we believe and how we live. As Paul wrote to Timothy, "All scripture is inspired by God, and is useful for teaching, for reproof, for correction, and for training in righteousness, so that everyone who belongs to God may be proficient, equipped for every good work" (NRSV). Notice that Paul said the scriptures are for everyone, not just for the trained professional clergy. As a pastor, my job was not to tell others what the Bible says but to help them interpret the Bible for themselves. That was an awesome responsibility, and it is an awesome responsibility for you—as you read and study the Bible, listen to sermons based on the Bible, and try to apply your understanding of the Bible to the way you think and live.

The problem is, rightly dividing the word of truth is not easy. Interpreting the Bible is complicated. All scripture is inspired by God, but not all scripture is of equal importance when it comes to applying it to our lives. For example, the antiquated dietary laws of the Old Testament are far less important to us than the teachings of Jesus in the New Testament. So, we make judgments about what parts of the Bible are most relevant for our situation. Being guided by the Scriptures is not so simple as randomly opening the Bible and placing a finger on a verse. Frankly, the Bible can be and has been used to justify almost any idea or behavior. As Shakespeare said, "[Even] the devil can cite Scripture for his purpose."[1]

Some years ago I came across a book written by Jim Hill and Rand Cheadle titled, *The Bible Tells Me So: Uses and Abuses of Holy Scripture*. Let me share this excerpt from the back cover to give you some idea of what the book is about:

> Does the Bible justify slavery—or its abolition? Support or oppose capital punishment? Prove the inferiority or superiority of one race or another? Justify hatred and persecution of homosexuals or advocate their acceptance just as they are? Depending on your point of view, the Bible does all these things—and more. Throughout history preachers, politicians, and pundits have selectively used the Bible to reach often contradictory conclusions on the great issues of morality and politics: from women's rights, abortion, and celibacy for the clergy, to war, civil rights, the environment, the separation of church and state—even appropriate hairstyles.

Here are some topics the book discusses where the Bible has been used and abused:

- to justify slavery
- to justify the abolishment of slavery
- to justify civil rights for African Americans
- to persecute the Jews
- to define the traditional role of women
- to provide sanctuary to political refugees
- to empower and liberate the poor
- to accuse and execute women as witches
- to support or oppose the ordination of women
- to oppose abortion
- to justify physical punishment of children
- to regulate clothing and hairstyles
- to argue the inferiority of black peoples
- to justify discrimination, intolerance, and violence toward homosexuals
- to provide spiritual strength and acceptance toward homosexuals
- to support or oppose capital punishment
- to define the terms of marriage
- to control the consumption of alcohol
- as part of a program of recovery from addition
- to forbid work and commerce on Sundays
- to justify or oppose prayer in public schools
- to oppose or embrace medical science
- to oppose or justify war
- to exploit or save the environment

As the book illustrates, the Bible can be used (or abused) to oppose or justify almost anything. Historian Bruce Gourley noted in his book, *A Capsule History of Baptists,* that before the Civil War, Christians in both the North and the South appealed to the Bible to justify their views against or for slavery. Gourley wrote: "Baptists in the North and South argued from scripture, with a literal biblical apologetic undergirding southern slavery and a broader, contextual interpretation of scripture empowering abolitionists." Using a literal biblical apologetic, Southern preachers would quote verses such as Colossians 3:22 and Ephesians 6:5: "Slaves, obey your masters." Using a broader contextual interpretation of scripture, Northern preachers would quote verses along the lines of Mark 12:31 and Matthew 22:39: "You shall love your neighbor as yourself."

In his second inaugural address President Abraham Lincoln noted that both North and South based their beliefs on the Bible: "Both read the same Bible and pray to the same God, and each invokes His aid against the other." So, scripture can be used to support almost any opinion. Our challenge is to rightly divide the word of truth so that we interpret the Bible correctly. And by correctly, I mean according to God's will. Of course, the big question is: How do we know God's will? For most Protestants, God's will is revealed in the written word, the Bible. But preeminently God's will is revealed in the living word, our Lord and Savior Jesus Christ. This is why we say that Jesus is the criterion by which we interpret scripture.

Some time ago, there was a popular slogan: "What would Jesus do?" sometimes shortened to the initials, "WWJD?" The idea was to measure all our actions and attitudes according to our understanding of the actions and attitudes of Jesus. Frankly, there are a lot of issues that the Bible does not specifically address. But the more we understand who Jesus was and what he said and did, the more we are guided in how we are to live.

A few years back, I was surprised to hear about an impromptu news conference with the head of the Roman Catholic Church, Pope Francis. During an extended question-and-answer session with reporters, the pope was asked about the church's attitude toward homosexuality. While not totally reversing the Roman Catholic Church's historic stance against homosexual behavior, the pope seemed to make the Church more open and welcoming than it has been in the past. Pope Francis told reporters "If someone is gay and he searches for the Lord and has good will, who am I to judge?"[2]

The pope did not quote any particular passage of scripture to illuminate his answer. But the very fact that he chose to answer the question, and that he answered the question in that way, suggests that he wants the Catholic Church to have a different attitude toward homosexuals than it has had in the past. "Who am I to judge?" the pope said. Perhaps even Pope Francis has asked himself the questions, "What would Jesus say? What would Jesus do?"

In the years since I first enrolled in seminary, I am still learning how to rightly divide the word of truth. I still don't have all the answers. But the more I come to know the one who is the answer, and the more I try to live like Jesus, the closer I come to discerning God's will for my life. I continue to struggle with the meaning of the Bible as I seek to rightly divide the word of truth. But as the Holy Spirit helps us to understand the inspired sacred writings, so the Holy Spirit also helps us apply the message to our lives.

JOHN WYCLIFFE: SCRIPTURE ALONE
(2 Tim. 3:14-17)

"This is the word of the Lord: *tu vero permane in his quae didicisti et credita sunt tibi sciens a quo didiceris.*" (2 Tim. 2:14).

What, you don't understand? This quote from 2 Timothy comes from the Bible that has been around for 1,600 years—the Latin Vulgate, first translated by Jerome. The Vulgate was the official Bible of the Roman Catholic Church from the 5th century up until the middle of the 20th century. If it's lasted that long, what's wrong with it? Oh, but you don't understand Latin, do you? You're not alone. Most people down through the centuries of the church have not understood Latin. In medieval England, for example, the average person didn't understand when the Bible was read in Latin. Even many of the priests in medieval England didn't understand Latin. This was in the 14th century, before the Renaissance, before the Reformation—the Middle Ages. This was the era of kings and castles, knights and cathedrals, lords and surfs, and a wealthy, almost all-powerful church.

Of course, when I say the church, I'm talking about the Roman Catholic Church. In the 14th century in Western Europe, it was the only church. In Greece, Turkey, Russia, and beyond, there was the Eastern Orthodox Church. The Roman Catholic Church of the 14th century was corrupt, by anyone's standards. There were two competing popes, and for a time even three popes, during what historians call "the Great Schism." The popes ruled more like political monarchs than spiritual leaders. Although sworn to celibacy, many of them had illegitimate children. High offices of the church were bought and sold or given as political plums. Bribery and the sale of indulgences lined the pockets of church officials. Many of the clergy were illiterate and immoral. Most knew little about the Bible. No wonder: The Bible was in Latin, and most priests were not fluent in Latin. If the clergy were biblically illiterate, you can imagine how much the laypeople knew about the Scriptures.

The 14th century has long been ignored by many historians because it was so bleak. The Black Plague was sweeping across much of Europe, in some places killing a third of the population. The 100 Years War engaged England and France in a century of senseless bloodshed. Wage controls in England drove the poor into ever more desperate poverty, leading to a Peasant's Revolt. It was into this dark and dismal time that a man named John Wycliffe appeared, with a message that shone forth a beacon of hope.

Wycliffe, a brilliant scholar who attained a Doctor of Theology at Oxford University, was appointed as chaplain to the king. Ordained a priest, he returned to Oxford to teach philosophy. But instead of joining in the abuses of the church and making himself wealthy at the expense of the poor, Wycliffe was sincere about his Christian faith. He was a devoted student of the Scriptures. On the basis of his study of the Bible, Wycliffe began to recognize that many of the teachings of the church were wrong. Instead of being grounded in Scripture, they were based on manmade traditions and ideas. Wycliffe began to critique the church.

He criticized such practices as the sale of indulgences, the concept of purgatory, the doctrine of transubstantiation, and even the authority of the pope. Most of all, Wycliffe believed that the Christian faith should be based on the Bible, and the Bible alone. He believed the most important thing a parish priest could do was to teach the Bible to his flock. He believed that if people could understand the Word of God, they could follow the Word of God. In contrast to the friars who preached sermons about legends and holy relics and tales of the saints, Wycliffe based his sermons on the Bible. His messages were filled, not with folklore or superstitions, but with scriptural exegesis.

To spread his message, Wycliffe began to train and send out preachers into the countryside to teach the people the Bible. As you might guess, John Wycliffe was not popular with the church authorities. He was banned from his teaching position at Oxford, and eventually he was tried as a heretic. Wycliffe was exiled to a remote parish church, but instead of silencing him, that banishment led to an even greater impact. With some of his students, Wycliffe began the work of translating the Bible from Latin into English. Working from a handwritten Latin manuscript that was more than a thousand years old, Wycliffe and his students translated the Bible into a language that people could understand.

John Wycliffe was condemned by the church, but he suffered a series of strokes and died of natural causes before the church could kill him. Thirty years later, however, he was posthumously condemned once again by a church council. Orders were given that his writings be destroyed, his bones be dug up and burned, and his ashes be thrown into a nearby river. Still, Wycliffe's influence and message continued to spread. Because of Wycliffe and those who followed after him, we can read the Bible in a language we can understand.

Now we can see how scripture is inspired by God, to instruct us for salvation through faith in Jesus Christ. Now we can see how these sacred writings show us how to live. Thanks to faithful Christians such as John Wycliffe, God's word is available to all of us who speak English. And Wycliffe Bible Translators are working even now to translate the Bible into every language on Earth. Thank God, his Word is available to us. What will we do with it?

QUESTIONS FOR DISCUSSION/REFLECTION

1. In what sense is Scripture "God-breathed"?
2. How can we use the Bible for "teaching, rebuking, correcting, and training in righteousness"?
3. What is the purpose of studying the Bible?
4. In what way is Jesus the criterion for interpreting the Bible?
5. How do we distinguish the cultural conditions of the Bible from the message of God's eternal purposes?

NOTES

[1] *The Merchant of Venice*, Act 1, Scene 3.
[2] Gene Robinson, "The Pope's Baby Steps on Gays," *Time*, August 12, 2013, 20.

About the Author

Bruce Salmon served for 33 years as pastor of Village Baptist Church in Bowie, Maryland. During that time, he preached almost 1,500 original Sunday morning sermons, including 295 sermons based on the letters of Paul. For the last 18 years of his ministry, he taught a Sunday morning pastor's class in which adults read and discussed entire books of the Bible. He also led winter, summer, and Lenten Sunday evening adult studies that covered various topics and Bible books, including the following:

- Introducing the New Testament
- The Sermon on the Mount
- The Life of Christ
- The Life of Paul
- The Passion of Jesus
- The Jesus of the Bible
- Genesis
- Exodus
- Joshua
- 1 Samuel
- 2 Samuel
- Isaiah

- Ezekiel
- Malachi
- Matthew
- Mark
- Luke
- John
- Acts
- Romans
- 2 Corinthians
- Hebrews
- James
- Revelation

A native of Fort Worth, Texas, Salmon received the Bachelor of Arts with a major in English from Baylor University and the Master of Divinity and Doctor of Ministry degrees from the Southern Baptist Theological Seminary. He also received the Master of Arts in Counseling Psychology from Bowie State University, with a specialization in Clinical Pastoral Counseling.

Salmon has served on several committees of the D.C. Baptist Convention and on several commissions of the Baptist World Alliance. In addition to this volume and others in the series *Spelunking Scripture*,* he is the author of *Storytelling in Preaching* (BSSB, 1988) and *Preaching for the Long Haul: A Case Study on Long-term Pastoral Ministry* (Nurturing Faith, 2019).

Salmon is husband to wife Linda, father to grown children Amy and Marc, father-in-law to Stacey, and grandfather to granddaughter Ford. In addition to studying the Bible, his interests include spectator sports, current events, music, museums, golf, and travel.

*For more information and blogs, visit www.spelunkingscripture.com.